THE BEST ACOUSTIC ROCK SHEET MUSIC

MW00700415

Alfred

Produced by
Alfred Music Publishing Co., Inc.
P.O. Box 10003
Van Nuys, CA 91410-0003
alfred.com

Printed in USA.

ISBN-10: 0-7390-8626-X
ISBN-13: 978-0-7390-8626-1

Cover photos:
Piano: © iStockphoto.com / JazzIRT • Figure: © Design Pics, Inc. / Alamy • Guitar: courtesy of the Martin Guitar Company

Alfred Cares. Contents printed on 100% recycled paper.

CONTENTS

50 WAYS TO LEAVE YOUR LOVER

Words and Music by
PAUL SIMON

Moderately ♩ = 104
Drum intro
N.C.
Em/G
B7
Cmaj7
B7(♭9)
B7
Em
B7
F♯dim7
B+
mp
Em/G
B7
Cmaj7
B7(♭9)
B7
Em
Am7
Em
Verse:
Em/G
D6
Cmaj7
B7(♭9)
B7
1. "The prob - lem is all in - side your head," she said to me;
2. She said, "It grieves me now to see you in such pain; I wish there was

Em
D♯dim7
F♯dim7
B+
Em
D6
"the an - swer is eas - y if you take it log - i - c'lly._ I'd like to help_ you in your
some - thing I could do to make you smile a - gain."_ I said, "I ap - pre - ci - ate that,
Cmaj7
B7(♭9)
B7
Em
Am7
Em
strug - gle to be free;_ there must be___ fif - ty ways_ to leave your lov - er."
and would you please ex - plain a - bout the___ fif - ty ways?"_
Em/G
D6
Cmaj7
B7(♭9)
She said, "It's real - ly not_ my hab - it to___ in - trude,___ fur - ther - more,_
She said, "Why don't we both_ just sleep___ on it___ to - night;___ and I be -
Em
D♯dim7
F♯dim7
B+
___ I hope my mean - ing won't be lost___ or mis - con - strued. But I'll re - peat_
lieve that in the morn - ing you'll be - gin___ to see_ the light." And then she kissed_

Em D6 Cmaj7 B7(♭9) Em Am7
my - self at the risk of be-ing crude; there must be fif - ty ways to leave your lov-
me and I real - ized she prob - a - bly was right; there must be fif - ty ways to leave your lov-
Em Am7 Em
er, fif - ty ways to leave your lov - er."
er, fif - ty ways to leave your lov - er.
You just slip out the
Chorus:
G B♭ C7
back, Jack; make a new plan, Stan; you don't need to be coy, Roy, just get your-self
mf
G B♭
free. Hop on the bus, Gus; you don't need to dis - cuss much; just drop off the

C7 G

key, Lee, and get your-self free. Oo, slip out the back, Jack; make a new

B♭ C7

plan, Stan; you don't need to be coy, Roy, you just lis-ten to

G B♭

me. Hop on the bus, Gus; you don't need to dis-cuss much; just drop off the

C7 G

1. 2.

key, Lee, and get your-self free.

fade out Drum figure

ALL I WANNA DO

Words and Music by
SHERYL CROW, WYN COOPER, KEVIN GILBERT,
BILL BOTTRELL and DAVID BAERWALD

Moderately ♩ = 116
B♭13
A13
B♭13
A13
B♭13
Spoken: Hit it!
This ain't no disco.
It ain't no country club either.
mf
A13
Verse 1:
E7
This is L.A.
1."All I wan - na do is have a lit - tle
C7
D9
fun be-fore I die," says the man next to me out of no - where,

E7
a - pro - pos of noth - ing. He says his name is Wil-liam, but I'm
C7
D9
sure he's Bill or Bil - ly or Mac or Bud - dy. 2. But he's
Verses 2 & 3:
E7
plain ug - ly to me and I won - der if he's ev - er had
3. See additional lyrics.
C7
D9
E7
a day of fun in his whole life. We are drink-ing beer at

C7
D9
noon on Tues-day in a bar__ that fac - es a gi - ant car wash. And the
E7
good peo - ple of the world are wash - ing their cars on their lunch break,
C7
D9
hos - ing and scrub-bing as best__ they can____ in skirts and suits.__
Bridge:
A13
B♭13
They drive__ their shin - y Dat - suns and Bu - icks

A13
B♭13
A13
back to the phone
com-pan-y, the re-cord store too._
Well, they're_ noth-ing like
Chorus:
E7
Bil-ly and me._ 'Cause all I wan-na
do
is have some
fun,___
I got a feel-
C7
D9
E7
- ing
I'm not the on - ly one.
All I wan-na
do
is have some fun,_
C7
D9
___
I got a feel - ing
I'm not the on - ly one.
All I wan-na

E7
To Coda
C7
do is have some fun, until the sun comes up o - ver
1. B7
E7
San - ta Mon - i - ca Boul - e - vard.
C7
D9
2. B7
San - ta Mon - i - ca Boul - e - vard.
E7
C7
D9
3

E7
C7
D9
Bridge:
A13
B♭13
A13
Oth-er - wise the bar is ours,
and the day and the night and the
B♭13
A13
car wash too.
The match-es and the Buds and the
B♭13
A13
D.S. 𝄋 al Coda
clean and dir - ty cars,
the sun and the moon. But all I wan - na

Coda
C7
D9
— I've got a feel - ing the par - ty has just be - gun. All I wan - na
E7
C7
do is have some fun, I won't tell you that you're the on -
D9
E7
- ly one. All I wan - na do is have some fun, un - til the
C7
D9
E7
sun comes up o - ver San - ta Mon - i - ca Boul - e - vard,

C7
D9
until the sun comes up over Santa Monica Boulevard.
E7
1. 2.
C7
D9
3. C7
B7(♯9)
E
rit.

Verse 3:
I like a good beer buzz early in the morning,
And Billy likes to peel the labels from his bottles of Bud
And shred them on the bar.
Then he lights every match in an oversized pack,
Letting each one burn down to his thick fingers
Before blowing and cursing them out.
And he's watching the Buds as they spin on the floor.
A happy couple enters the bar dancing dangerously close to one another.
The bartender looks up from his want ads.
(To Chorus:)

BIG YELLOW TAXI

Words and Music by
JONI MITCHELL

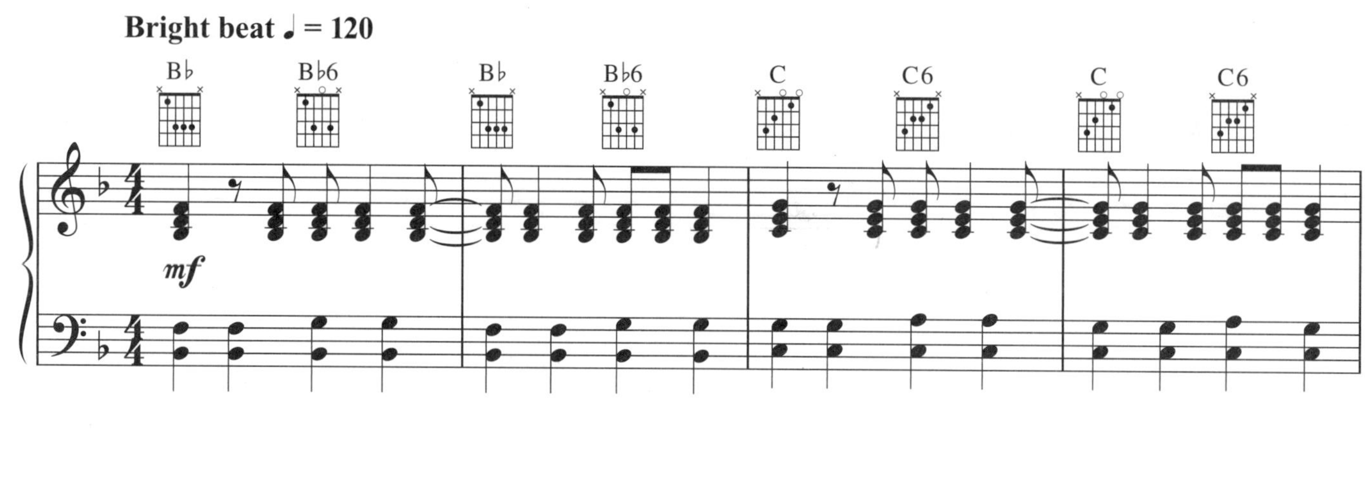
Bright beat ♩ = 120
B♭
B♭6
B♭
B♭6
C
C6
C
C6
mf

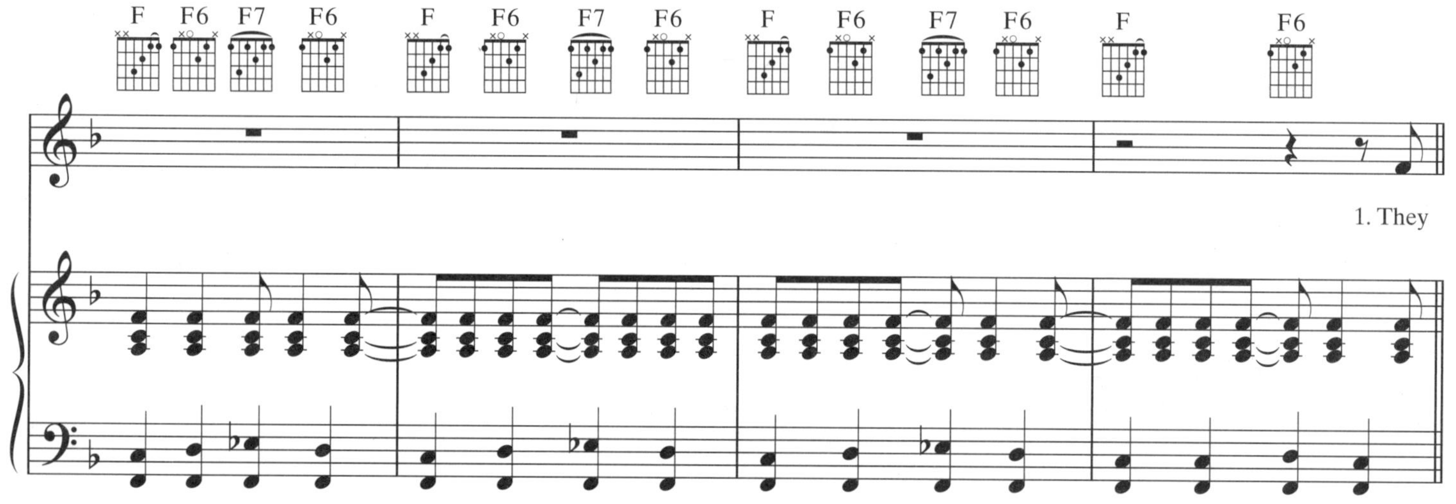
F
F6
F7
F6
F
F6
F7
F6
F
F6
F7
F6
F
F6
1. They

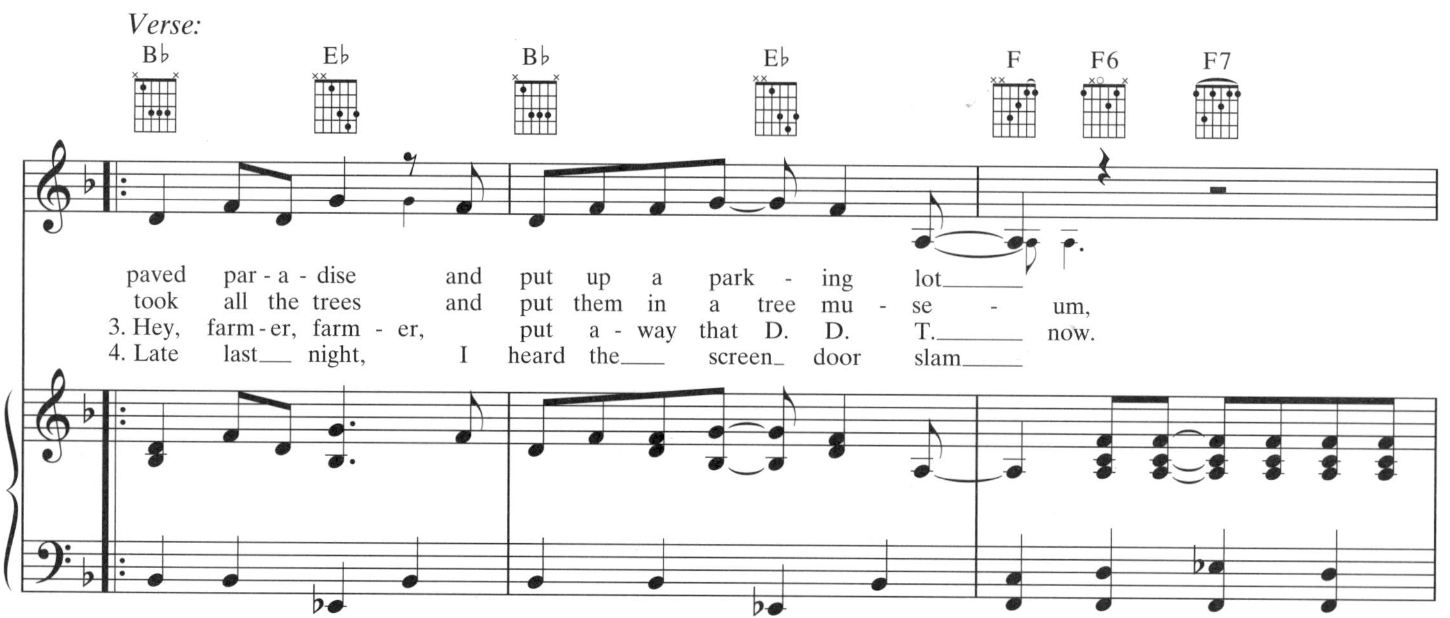
Verse:
B♭
E♭
B♭
E♭
F
F6
F7
paved par - a - dise and put up a park - ing lot
took all the trees and put them in a tree mu - se - um,
3. Hey, farm - er, farm - er, put a - way that D. D. T. now.
4. Late last night, I heard the screen door slam

F F6 F7 B♭ E♭ C
with a pink ho - tel, a bou-tique, and a
and they charged all the peo-ple a dol-lar and a half just to
Give me spots on my ap-ples, but leave me the birds and the
and a big yel-low tax-i took a-way my old
F F6 F7 F6 F F6
swing - ing hot spot.
see 'em.
bees, please!
man.
Chorus:
F F7
Don't it al - ways seem to go that you don't know what you've got
B♭ E♭ C
till it's gone? They paved par - a - dise and put up a park - ing lot.

1.2.3.
F F6 F7 F6 F F6 F F6 F F6 F7 F6
(Woo, bop bop bop bop.) Woo, bop
F F6 F F6
4.
F F6 F7 F6 F F6 F F6
bop bop bop.)
2. They
(Woo, bop bop bop bop.)
Chorus:
F F7
Don't it al - ways seem to go that you don't know what you've got till it's gone? They
Repeat ad lib. and fade
B♭ E♭ C F F6 F7 F6 F F6 F F6
paved par - a - dise and put up a park - ing lot. They
a tempo

BLOWIN' IN THE WIND

Words and Music by
BOB DYLAN

Moderately, in 2 ♩ = 86
Guitar Capo 7
Piano
G
D
Verse:
C
C/B
G
G/F♯
mf
1. How man - y roads must a man
2.3. See additional lyrics
D
A
G
D
walk down be - fore you call him a man?
How man - y seas must the white

D
G
C
C/B
A
D
G
G/F♯
dove sail before she sleeps in the sand?
Yes, and how many times must the cannon balls fly before they're for - ev - er banned?
Chorus:
The an - swer, my friend, is

G
C
C/B
D
D
G
G/F♯
A
blow-in' in the wind.
The an - swer is blow-in' in the wind.
C
C/B
D
G
C
G
G/F♯
A
D
G
1.2.
C/B
D
G
G/F♯
A
D
2.3. Yes, and
3.
C
C/B
D
G
G
G/F♯
A
D

Verse 2:
Yes, and how many years can a mountain exist
Before it is washed to the sea?
Yes, and how many years can some people exist
Before they're allowed to be free?
Yes, and how many times can a man turn his head
And pretend that he just doesn't see?
(To Chorus:)

Verse 3:
Yes, and how many times must a man look up
Before he can see the sky?
Yes, and how many ears must one man have
Before he can hear people cry?
Yes, and how many deaths will it take till he knows
That too many people have died?
(To Chorus:)

BLACK WATER

Words and Music by
PATRICK SIMMONS

Moderately
Am7
D
Am7
D
Well, I
mp
R.H.
Am7
D
Am7
D
built me a raft ___ and she's read - y for float - in';
Am7
D
Am7
D
ol' Mis - sis - sip pi, ___ she's call - in' my name. ___

Am7
D
Am7
D
Cat - fish are jump-in', that pad-dle wheel thump - in', black
Am7
D
Am7
D
wa-ter keeps roll - in' on past just the same.
G
Old black wa - ter, keep on roll - in',
Bb
Mis - sis-sip-pi moon, won't you
G
Old black wa - ter, keep on roll - in',
keep on shin - in' on me? Mis -

Bb
G
sis-sip-pi moon, won't you keep on shin - in' on me?
Old black wa - ter,
keep on roll - in',
Bb
Mis - sis-sip-pi moon, won't you keep on shin - in' on
A
Em7
A
Em7
me? Yeah, keep on shin - in' your light, gon-na make
A
Em7
A
Em7
ev - 'ry - thing, pret-ty ma - ma, gon-na make ev - 'ry-thing all right.

D
Am7
And I ain't got no wor - ries 'cause I
D
Am7
A
Em7
ain't in no hur - ry at all.
A
Am7
D
Am7
To Coda
D
Am7
D
Well, if it rains, I don't care, don't make no

Am7 D Am7
dif - fer - ence to me; just take that street - car that's go -
D Am7 D Am7
in' up - town. Yeah, I'd like to hear some fun - ky
D Am7 D
Dix - ie - land and dance a hon - ky - tonk, and I'll be
Am7 D Am7 D
D. S. 𝄋 al Coda
buy - in' ev - 'ry - bod - y drinks all 'roun'.

Coda
Repeat and fade
D
Am7
D
I'd like to hear some fun - ky Dix. - ie - land, pret-ty ma -
Am7
D
Am7
ma, come and take me by the hand, by the hand. Take me by the
I want to hon-ky-tonk, hon-ky -
D
Am7
D
hand, pret-ty ma-ma, come and dance with your dad-dy all night long. I'd like to
tonk, hon-ky-tonk with you all night long.

BOULEVARD OF BROKEN DREAMS

Words by
BILLIE JOE

Music by
GREEN DAY

Moderately slow ♩ = 86

F5 A♭5 E♭5 B♭5

mf

F5 A♭5 E♭5 B♭5

Verses 1 & 2:

Fm A♭ E♭ B♭

1. I walk a lone - ly road, the on - ly one that I___ have ev - er known._
2. I'm walk - ing down the line that di - vides me___ some - where in my___

Fm
Ab4
Eb6
Bb
Don't know where it goes, but it's home to me and I walk a - lone.
mind. On the bor - der - line of the edge and where I walk a - lone.
Fm
Ab4
Eb6
Bb
Fm
Ab4
Eb6
Bb
I walk this emp - ty street on the bou - le - vard of bro - ken dreams,
Read be - tween the lines of what's f***ed up and ev - ery - thing's al -
Fm
Ab4
Eb6
Bb
where the cit - y sleeps and I'm the on - ly one and I walk a - lone.
right. Check my vi - tal signs and know I'm still a - live and I walk a - lone.

Fm
A♭
E♭
B♭
Fm
A♭
I walk a - lone, I walk a - lone.
Chorus:
E♭
B♭
A♭/C
D♭
A♭
I walk a - lone, I walk a...
My shad - ow's the on -
E♭
Fm
D♭
A♭
ly one that walks be - side me.
My shal - low heart's
E♭
Fm
D♭
A♭
the on - ly thing that's beat - ing.
Some - times I wish

E♭
Fm
D♭
A♭
To Coda
some - one out there will find me.
'Til then I walk
C
N.C.
B♭
a - lone.
Ah.
Ah.
Ah.
Ah.
1.
2.
A♭/C
I walk a - lone, I walk a…
(Gtr. solo…

E♭
Fm
D♭
A♭
E♭
Fm
D♭
A♭
C
N.C.
...end solo)
Verse 3:
Fm
A♭
E♭
B♭
3. I walk this emp - ty street on the bou - le - vard of bro - ken dreams,

D.S. 𝄋 al Coda
Fm
A♭
E♭
B♭
A♭/C
where the cit - y sleeps and I'm the on - ly one and I walk a…
Coda
C
a - lone.
F5
D♭
E♭2
B♭/D
1.2.3.
A♭5
E5
4.
A♭5
E5

BRIDGE OVER TROUBLED WATER

Words and Music by
PAUL SIMON

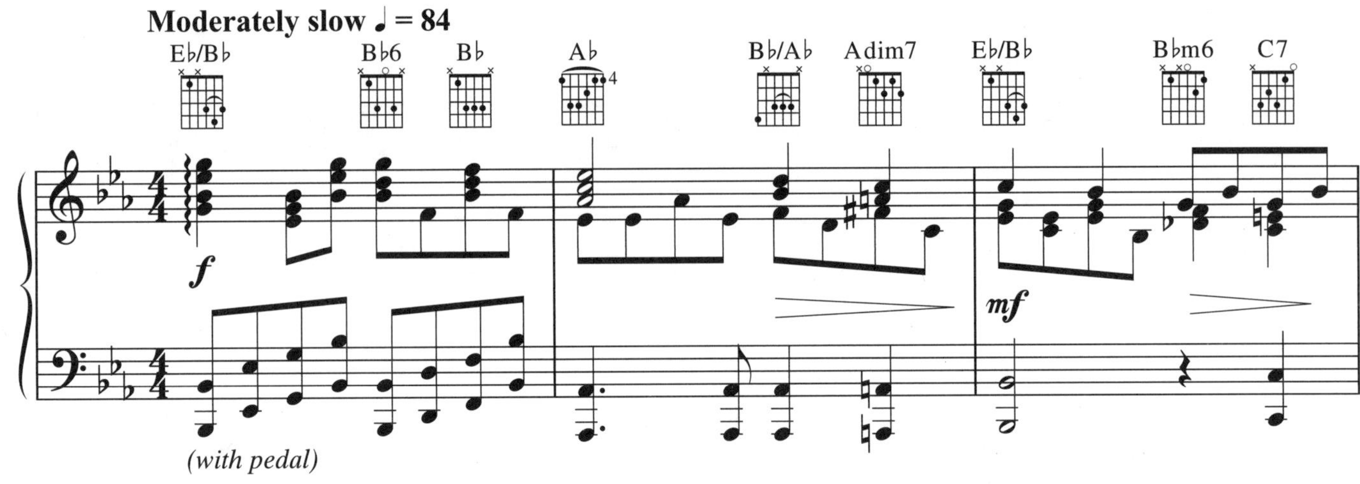
Moderately slow ♩ = 84
E♭/B♭
B♭6
B♭
A♭
B♭/A♭
Adim7
E♭/B♭
B♭m6
C7
f
mf
(with pedal)

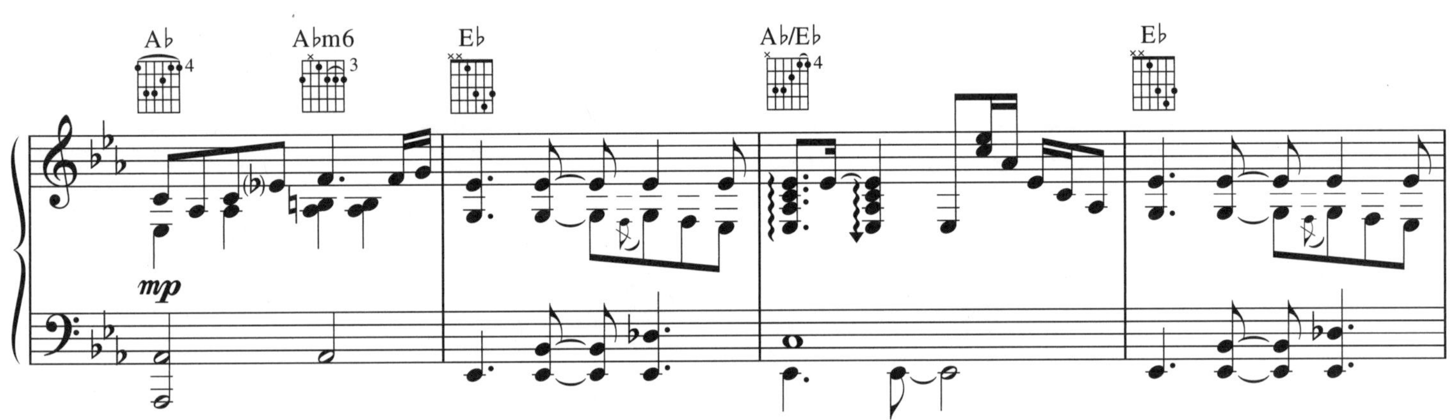
A♭
A♭m6
E♭
A♭/E♭
E♭
mp

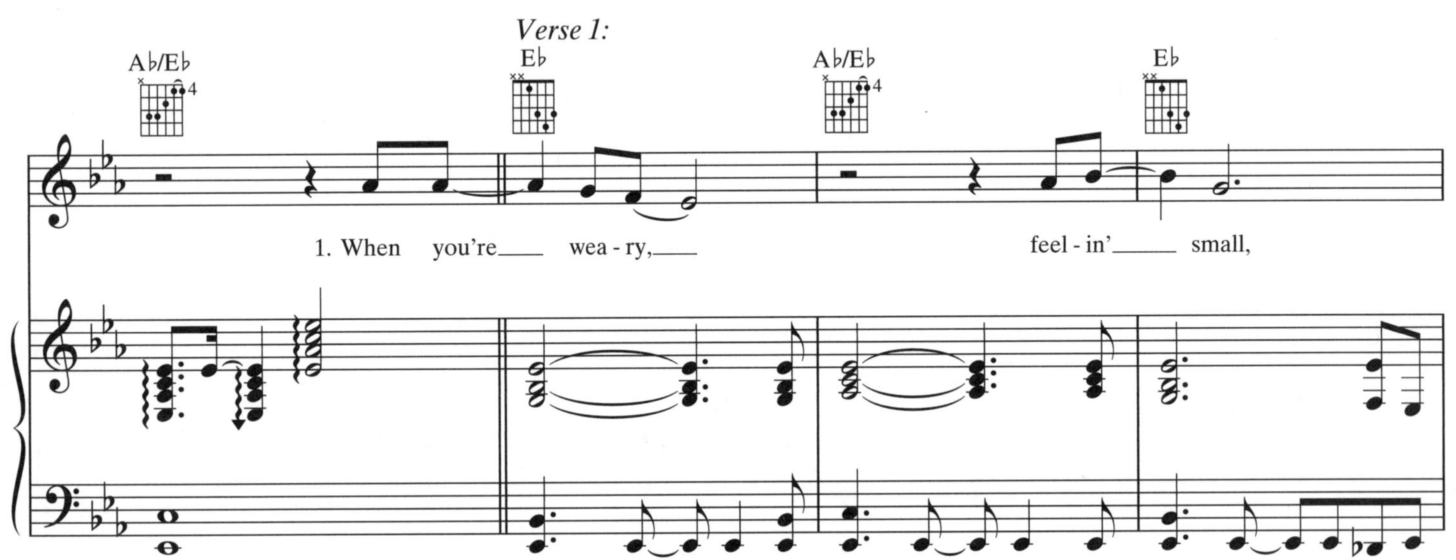
A♭/E♭
Verse 1:
E♭
A♭/E♭
E♭
1. When you're___ wea - ry,___ feel - in'___ small,

Ab Db Ab Eb Ebmaj7 Fm7 Eb Ab
when tears are in your eyes, I will dry them all.
Eb Ab Eb Bb/D Cm7 Bb7
I'm on your side, oh,
mf
Eb Ebmaj7/D Eb7/Db Eb7 Fm7 Eb7/G
when times get rough, and friends just
Ab F7 Bb Bb/D Eb Bb Ab Bb/Ab Adim7
can't be found, like a bridge o - ver

Eb/Bb C7sus C7 Ab Bdim7 Cm Eb Bb
trou-bled wa-ter, I will lay me down. Like a
Ab Bb/Ab Adim7 Eb/Bb C7sus C7 Ab Bdim7
bridge o - ver trou-bled wa-ter, I will lay me down.
Eb Eb7 Ab7 Eb
mp
Ab/Eb Eb Ab/Eb
2. When you're

Verse 2:

E♭ A♭/E♭ E♭

down and out, when you're on the street,

A♭ D♭ A♭ E♭ E♭maj7 Fm7

when eve - ning falls so hard, I will

E♭ A♭ E♭ A♭ E♭ B♭/D Cm7

com - fort you. I'll take your

B♭7 E♭ E♭maj7/D

part, oh, when dark - ness comes,

mf

E♭7/D♭
E♭
D♭/F
E♭7/G
A♭
F7
B♭
E♭
B♭
and pain is all a - round, like a
A♭
B♭/A♭
Adim7
E♭/B♭
C7sus
C7
A♭
G7/B
bridge o - ver trou-bled wa - ter, I will lay me down.
Cm
E♭
B♭
A♭
B♭/A♭
Adim7
E♭/B♭
C7sus
Cm7
Like a bridge o - ver trou-bled wa - ter,
A♭
G7(♯5)
G7
Cm
Cm/B
Cm/B♭
F6
F6/E
F6/E♭
I will lay me down.

Eb/Bb
Bb6
Ab
Cm
Ab
Abm
mf
Eb
Ab/Eb
Eb
mp
Ab/Eb
Eb
Eb7
Ab/Eb
3. Sail on,
Verse 3:
Eb
Ab/Eb
Eb
sil - ver girl,
sail on by.

A♭
D♭
A♭
E♭
Fm7
Your time has come to shine.___ All your
E♭
A♭
E♭
A♭
E♭
B♭/D
Cm
dreams are on their_ way.
See how they
B♭
E♭
E♭maj7/D♭
shine.___
Oh,___ if you need a friend,___
mf
E♭7/D♭
E♭
D♭/F
E♭7/G
A♭
F7
B♭
E♭
I'm sail - ing right be - hind,___ like a
f

A♭ B♭/A♭ Adim7 E♭/B♭ C7sus Cm A♭ G7(♯5)/B G7/B
bridge o - ver trou-bled wa - ter, I will ease your mind.
Cm E♭ B♭ A♭ B♭/A♭ Adim7 E♭/B♭ Cm7
Like a bridge o - ver trou - bled wa - ter,
A♭ G7(♯5) Cm Cm/B Cm/B♭ F6 F6/E F6/E♭
I will ease your mind.
E♭/B♭ B♭ A♭ Cm A♭ A♭m E♭
molto rit.

BOTH SIDES NOW

Words and Music by
JONI MITCHELL

Moderately, with a light beat
A♭
D♭
mp
Verse:
Cm
1. Bows and flows of an - gel hair and ice - cream cas - tles
2. Moons and Junes and Fer - ris wheels, the diz - zy danc - ing
3. Tears and fears and feel - ing proud to say, "I love you,"
B♭m
in the air, and feath - er can - yons ev - 'ry - where,
way you feel, when ev - 'ry fair - y tale comes real,
right out loud. Dreams and schemes and cir - cus crowds,

E♭ A♭ D♭ A♭
I've looked at clouds that way. But now they on - ly block the sun,_ they
I've looked at love that way. But now it's just an - oth - er show,_ you
I've looked at life that way. But now old friends are act - ing strange,_ they
Cm D♭ A♭ D♭
rain and snow on ev - 'ry - one._ So man - y things I
leave 'em laugh - ing when you go._ And if you care, don't
shake their heads, they say I've changed._ But some-thing's lost, but
B♭m E♭
would have done, but clouds got in my way. I've
let them know, don't give your - self a - way. I've
some-thing's gained in liv - ing ev - 'ry day. I've
Chorus:
A♭ D♭ A♭ D♭ A♭
looked at clouds_ from both_ sides now,_ from up and down_ and
looked at love_ from both_ sides now,_ from give and take_ and
looked at life_ from both_ sides now,_ from win and lose_ and

D♭ A♭ Cm D♭ A♭
still____ some - how it's cloud il - lu - sions I re - call; I
still____ some - how it's love's il - lu - sions I re - call; I
still____ some - how it's life's il - lu - sions I re - call; I
A♭/C D♭/E♭ E♭
real - ly____ don't know clouds____ at____
real - ly____ don't know love____ at____
real - ly____ don't know life____ at____
A♭ D♭ A♭ D♭ A♭ D♭
all.____
all.____
all.____
1.2.
3.
Repeat and fade
A♭ D♭ A♭ D♭ A♭ D♭ A♭ D♭

CAT'S IN THE CRADLE

Words and Music by
HARRY CHAPIN and SANDY CHAPIN

Moderately, with a 2 feel 𝅗𝅥 = 72
Guitar Capo 8 → A5
Em7
Piano → F5
Cm7
mp
(with pedal)
A
F
1. My
Verses 1–3:
A
F
C
A♭
D
B♭
child ar - rived__ just the oth - er day, he came to the world in the
son turned_ ten just the oth - er day, he said, "Thanks for the ball, Dad, come
came from col - lege just the oth - er day, so much like a man, I just
A
F
C
A♭
u - su - al way.__ But there were planes to catch__ and bills to pay.__
on, let's__ play.__ Can you teach me to throw?"_ I said, "Not to - day,__ I've got a
had to say,______ "Son, I'm proud of you.____ Can you sit for a while?"___ He

D
A
G
G/F#
B♭
F
E♭
E♭/D
He learned to walk while I was a - way. And he was talk - in' 'fore I knew it and
lot to do." He said, "That's o - kay." And he, he walked a - way, but his
shook his head and he said with a smile, "What I'd real - ly like, Dad, is to
Em7
Em/D
C
Em/B
1.2.
A
Cm7
Cm/B♭
A♭
Cm/G
F
as he grew, he'd say, "I'm gon - na be like you, Dad. You
smile nev - er dimmed._ It said, "I'm gon - na be like him, yeah. You
bor - row the car keys. See you lat - er. Can I
C
Em/B
A
To Next Strain
A♭
Cm/G
F
know I'm gon - na be like you."
know I'm gon - na be like him."
And the
cresc.
3.
A
Chorus:
A
F
F
have them, please?"
And the cat's in the cra - dle and the
cresc.
mf

G
C
D
E♭
A♭
B♭
sil - ver spoon,
Lit - tle Boy Blue and the man in the moon.
A
G
C
Em/B
F
E♭
A♭
Cm/G
1.2. "When you com - in' home, Dad?" "I don't know when, but we'll get to - geth - er then,
3. "When you com - in' home, Son?" "I don't know when, but we'll get to - geth - er then,
A
C
Em/B
1.2.
A
F
A♭
Cm/G
F
Son. You know we'll have a good time then."
Dad. You know we'll have a good time
A5
F5
mp

Em7
A
D.S. 𝄋
3.
A
Cm7
F
F
2. My
then."
3. Well, he
F
G
Em
A
D♭
E♭
Cm
F
F
G
Em
A
D♭
E♭
Cm
F
Verse 4:
A
F
4. I've long since re - tired, my

C
A♭
D
B♭
A
F
son's moved a - way. I called him up just the oth - er day.
C
A♭
I said, "I'd like to see you if you don't mind." He said, "I'd
D
B♭
A
F
love to, Dad, if I could find the time. You see, my
G
E♭
G/F#
E♭/D
Em7
Cm7
Em/D
Cm/B♭
C
A♭
Em/B
Cm/G
new job's a has - sle and the kids have the flu, but it's sure nice talk - in' to

A C Em/B A
F A♭ Cm/G F
you, Dad. It's been sure nice talk - in' to you."
G G/F♯ Em7 Em/D
E♭ E♭/D Cm7 Cm/B♭
And as I hung up the phone,_ it oc - curred to me,_ he'd
mp
C Em/B A C Em/B
A♭ Cm/G F A♭ Cm/G
grown up just like me. My boy was just like
A
F
Chorus:
me. And the cat's in the cra - dle and the
mf

G C D
E♭ A♭ B♭
sil - ver spoon, Lit - tle Boy Blue and the man in the moon.
A G C Em/B
F E♭ A♭ Cm/G
"When you com - in' home, Son?" "I don't know when, but we'll get to - geth - er then,
A C Em/B A A5
F A♭ Cm/G F F5
Dad. We're gon - na have a good time then."
rit.
a tempo mp
Em7 A
Cm7 F
poco rit.

CAN'T FIND MY WAY HOME

All gtrs. in Drop D tuning:
⑥ = D ③ = G
⑤ = A ② = B
④ = D ① = E

Words and Music by
STEVE WINWOOD

Moderately slow ♩ = 88
C2
G/B
Gm/B♭
D/A
mf
F
G
D
C2
G/B
Gm/B♭
D/A
F
G
D
1. Come
Verse 1:
C2
G/B
Gm/B♭
D/A
down off your throne and leave your bod-y a-lone.

F G D

Some - bod - y must change.

C2 G/B Gm/B♭ D/A

You are the rea - son I've been wait - ing so long.

F G D

Some - bod - y holds the key. Well, I'm

Chorus 1:

G/B Asus A

near the end, I just ain't got the time,

D
Em
and I'm wast - ed and I
G
F♯m
Em
D
can't find my way home.
C2
G/B
Gm/B♭
D/A
F
G
D
C2
G/B
Gm/B♭
D/A
Ooh.

F
G
D
Ooh.
2. Come
Verse 2:
C2
G/B
Gm/B♭
D/A
down on your own and leave your bod-y a-lone.
F
G
D
Some-bod-y must change.
C2
G/B
Gm/B♭
D/A
You are the rea-son I've been wait-ing all these years.

F
G
D
Some - bod - y holds the key.
Well, I'm
Chorus 2:
G/B
Asus
A
near the end, I just ain't got the time,
D
Em
oh, and I'm wast - ed and I
G
F♯m
Em
D
can't find my way home.

Interlude:

C2
G/B
Gm/B♭
D/A
F
G
D
C2
G/B
Ooh,
Gm/B♭
D/A
F
G
but I
can't
find
my
way
D
C2
G/B
Gm/B♭
D/A
home.
Ah,
but I

F
G
D
can't find my way home.
Ooh,
C2
G/B
Gm/B♭
D/A
but I can't
F
G
D
find my way home.
Ah,
C2
G/B
Gm/B♭
D/A
dee, doo,
but I

F
G
D
can't find my way home.
Still I can't
find my way home.
And I
ain't done nothing wrong,
but I
can't find my way home.
poco rit.

CRAZY LOVE

Words and Music by
VAN MORRISON

Slowly ♩ = 72
Verses 1 & 2:
A
C♯m
D
A
1. I can hear her heart-beat for a thou - sand miles, and the
fine sense of hu - mor when I'm feel - in' low down. And when
mp
(with pedal)

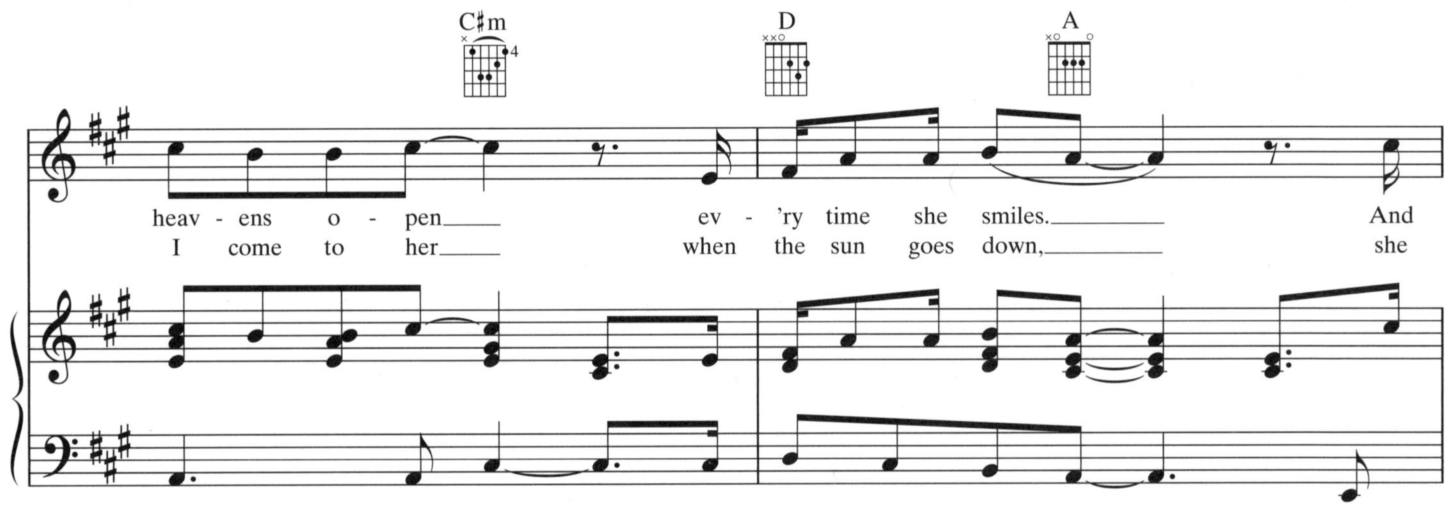
C♯m
D
A
heav - ens o - pen ev - 'ry time she smiles. And
I come to her when the sun goes down, she

C♯m
D
A
when I come to her, that's where I be - long. Yes, I'm
takes a - way my trou - ble, takes a-way my grief. Takes a -

C♯m
D
A
running to her like a river's song.
way my heart-ache in the night like a thief.
She gives me
Chorus:
E/G♯
F♯m
F♯m/E
D
E
A
love, love, love, love, cra - zy love.
She gives me love, love, love, love,
1.
2.
Bridge:
cra - zy love.
2. She's got a cra - zy love.
And I need her in the
day - time,
and I need her in the night.

E
D
A
F♯m
And I want to throw my arms a-round her and
Bm7
E
A
E
kiss her, hug her, kiss her, hug her tight.
3. And when
Verse 3:
A
C♯m
D
A
I'm re-turn-ing from so far a-way, she gives me
C♯m
D
A
such sweet lov-in', bright-ens up my day. Yeah, it

A
C♯m
D
A
makes me right - eous
and it makes me whole.
C♯m
D
A
And it makes me mel - low
down to my soul.
She gives me
Chorus:
E/G♯
F♯m
F♯m/E
D
E
A
E/G♯
F♯m
F♯m/E
love, love, love, love,
cra - zy love.
She gives me
love, love, love, love,
1.
2.
D
A
D
A
cra - zy love.
She's got a
cra - zy love.

CREEP

Words and Music by
THOMAS YORKE, JONATHAN GREENWOOD,
COLIN GREENWOOD, EDWARD O'BRIEN, PHILIP SELWAY,
ALBERT HAMMOND and MIKE HAZELWOOD

♩ = 93

G
3fr
B
7fr
p
Ped.

5

C 8fr

Cm 8fr

1. When you were here be - fore,

Pedal cont. sim.

9

G 3fr

B 7fr

(2.) (hurts,) could-n't look you in the eye,

I want to have con - trol.

C
8fr
12
you're just like an an - gel,
your skin makes me cry.
I want a per-fect bo - dy,
I want a per-fect soul.
Cm
8fr
G
3fr
15
You float like a fea - ther
I want you to no - tice
B
7fr
18
in a beau-ti-ful world.
when I'm not a-round.
I wish I was spe-
You're so fuck-ing spe-

C
Cm
Muted Guitar
21
- cial, you're so fuck - ing spe - cial.
- cial, I wish I was spe - cial.
But I'm a creep,
G
B
25
I'm a weir - do.
f
C
28
What the hell am I do - ing here?
I don't be - long
1.
2.
Cm
Cm
31
here.
2. I don't care if it hurts, -long here,
oh, oh.
mp

G
3fr
B
7fr
She's
run - ning out
the door.
ff
C
8fr
Cm
8fr
She's
run - ning out,
she
run,
run,
run,
run,
G
3fr
B
7fr
B7
7fr
C
8fr
Cm
8fr
run.
What-e-ver makes you hap -

G
B
3fr
7fr
51
-py, what-e-ver you want.
You're so fuck-ing spe-
p
C
Cm
8fr
55
-cial, I wish I was spe-cial.
But I'm a creep,
59
I'm a weir-do.
What the hell am I do-ing here?
mp
63
rit.
I don't be-long here.
I don't be-long here.

DESPERADO

Words and Music by
DON HENLEY and GLENN FREY

Slowly ♩ = 72
G
G7
C
Cm6
G
Em
mf
(with pedal)
A7
D
G
G7
C
Cm6
Des-per-a - do, why don't you come to your sens - es? You been
a tempo
mp
G
Em
A7
D7
G
G7
out rid - in' fenc - es for so long now. Oh, you're a hard one, I know that
C
Cm6
G/D
G+/D♯
Em
you got your rea - sons, these things that are pleas - in' you can
cresc.

A7
D7
G
D/F♯
Em
Bm7
hurt you some - how.
Don't you draw the queen of dia - monds, boy, she'll
mf
C
G
Em
C
beat you if she's a - ble.
You know the queen of hearts is al - ways your best
G
D/F♯
Em7
Bm7
bet.
Now it seems to me some fine things have been
C
G
Em
A7
Am7/D
D
laid up - on your ta - ble, but you on - ly want the ones that you can't get.
Des - per - a -
poco rit. decresc.

G
G7
C
G/B
Am7
G
D/F♯
Em
do, oh, you ain't get-tin' no youn - ger, your pain and your hun - ger,
a tempo
A7
D7
G
G7
they're driv - in' you home. And free-dom, oh, free-dom, well, that's just
C
G/B
Am7
G/D
G+/D♯
Em
A7
D7
some peo-ple talk - in'. Your pris - on is walk - in' through this world all a - lone.
G
D/F♯
Em
Bm7
Don't your feet get cold in the win - ter - time? The
cresc.
mf

C
G
Em
C
sky won't snow and the sun won't shine.
It's hard to tell
the night - time from the day.
G
D
Em7
Bm7
You're los - in' all
your highs
and lows.
Ain't it
C
G
Am7
C/D
D
fun-ny how the feel - ing goes
a - way?
Des - per - a -
G
G7
C
Cm6
G
D/F♯
Em
do, why don't you come to your sens - es?
Come down from your fenc - es,
3

A7
D7
G
G7
3
o - pen the gate.
It may be
rain - in',
but there's a
C
C6
G
D/F♯
Em
C
G/B
Am7
Am7/D
rain-bow a - bove_you.
You bet-ter
let some-bod-y love you,
you__ bet-ter
G/D
G+/D♯
Em
Am7/D
let some-bod - y
love__
you______
be - fore
it's
too________________________________
mp
G
G7
C
Cm6
G(9)
late.
a tempo
rit.

EVERYBODY HURTS

Words and Music by
WILLIAM BERRY, MICHAEL STIPE
MICHAEL MILLS and PETER BUCK

Moderately, with motion
D
G
D
mf
G
D
long.
When the day is long
When your day is night a
If you're on your own
G
D
lone,
and the night,
in this life,
the night is yours a - lone,
if you feel like let - ting go,
the days and nights are long
G
D
when you're sure you've had e -
when you think you've had too
when you think you've had too

G
D
nough of this life, well, hang on.
much of this life, well, hang on
much of this life to hang on.
G
Em
A
Don't let your - self go,
'cause eve - ry - bod - y hurts.
Well, eve - ry - bod - y hurts some -
Em
A
eve - ry - bod - y cries
Take com - fort in your friends.
times, eve - ry - bod - y cries.

Em
To Coda
1 A
no chord
and eve - ry - bod - y hurts some -
Eve - ry - bod - y
And eve - ry - bod - y
D
G
- times.
Some - times eve - ry - thing is
D
G
wrong.
Now it's time to sing a -
2 A
F#7
hurts.
Don't throw your hand.

Bm
F#7
Bm
Oh, no.
F#7
Bm
Don't throw your hand.
C
G
If you feel like you're a - lone,
C
G/B
Am
D.S. al Coda
no chord
no, no, no, you are not a - lone.

CODA
A
no chord
D
hurts some - times.
G
D
G
And eve - ry - bod - y hurts some - times. So, hold
D7
G
on, hold on. Hold
D7
G
Repeat and Fade
on, hold on. Hold

FRIEND OF THE DEVIL

Words by
ROBERT HUNTER

Music by
JERRY GARCIA and JOHN DAWSON

Moderately fast Country beat
G
C
G
mp
I lit out from Re-no, I was trailed by twen-ty hounds.
ran in-to the dev-il, babe, he loaned me twen-ty bills. I
Did-n't get to sleep that night till the morn-ing came a-round.
spent the night in U-tah in a cave, up in the hills.

D
Am
Set out run-nin' but I take my time, a friend of the dev-il is a friend of mine. If
D
Am
I get home be-fore day - light, I just might get some sleep to-
D
1.
2.
night.
I
I
G
C
G
ran down to the lev - ee but the dev - il caught me there. He

C
G
took my twen-ty dol - lar bill — and he van-ished in the air. —
D
Am
Set out run-nin' but I take my time, — a friend of the dev - il is a
D
Am
friend of mine. — If I get home — be-fore — day - light, — I just might get some
Third time to Coda
D
sleep to - night. —

D
Got two rea - sons why I cry a - way each lone - ly night.
mf
C
The first one's named Sweet Anne Mar - ie and she's
D
my heart's de - light.
Sec - ond one is pris - on, ba - by, the
Am
sher - iff's on my trail, and if he catch - es up with me I

C
D
spend my life in jail.
G
C
Got a wife in Chi-no, babe, and one in Cher-o-kee.
G
First one says she's got my child, but
1.
2.
D. S. al Coda
C
G
G
Coda
D
it don't look like me. me.
night.

FAITHFULLY

Words and Music by
JONATHAN CAIN

Slow rock ♩ = 66
B
G♯m
mf
B/F♯
E
1. High - way,
B
G♯m
run in - to the mid - night sun.
life un - der the big - top world.

E B

Wheels go 'round_ and 'round,__ you're on my mind.
We all need__ the clowns__ to make us smile.

Rest - less hearts sleep a -
Through space and time, al - ways an -

G♯m E

lone to - night,__ send - in' all__ my love__ a - long the
oth - er__ show.__ Won - d'ring where_ I am,__ lost with -

B/F♯ F♯ E G♯m

wire.________ They say that the road ain't no__ place to start a fam-
out you.__ And be - in' a - part ain't eas - y on this love

B
E
G♯m
'ly.
af - fair.
Right down the line it's been you and me.
Two strang - ers learn to fall in love a -
B
E
G♯m
gain.
And lov - in' a mu - sic man ain't al - ways what it's
I get the joy of re - dis -
B
F♯
D♯m
s'pposed to be.
cov - 'ring you.
Oh, girl, you stand by
F♯
C♯m
B/D♯
me.
I'm for - ev - er yours,

E
B
faith - ful - ly.
G♯m
B/F♯
1.
2. Cir - cus
2.
Oh,
oh,
1.– 4.
5.
oh.

FALLING SLOWLY

Words and Music by
GLEN HANSARD and
MARKETA IRGLOVA

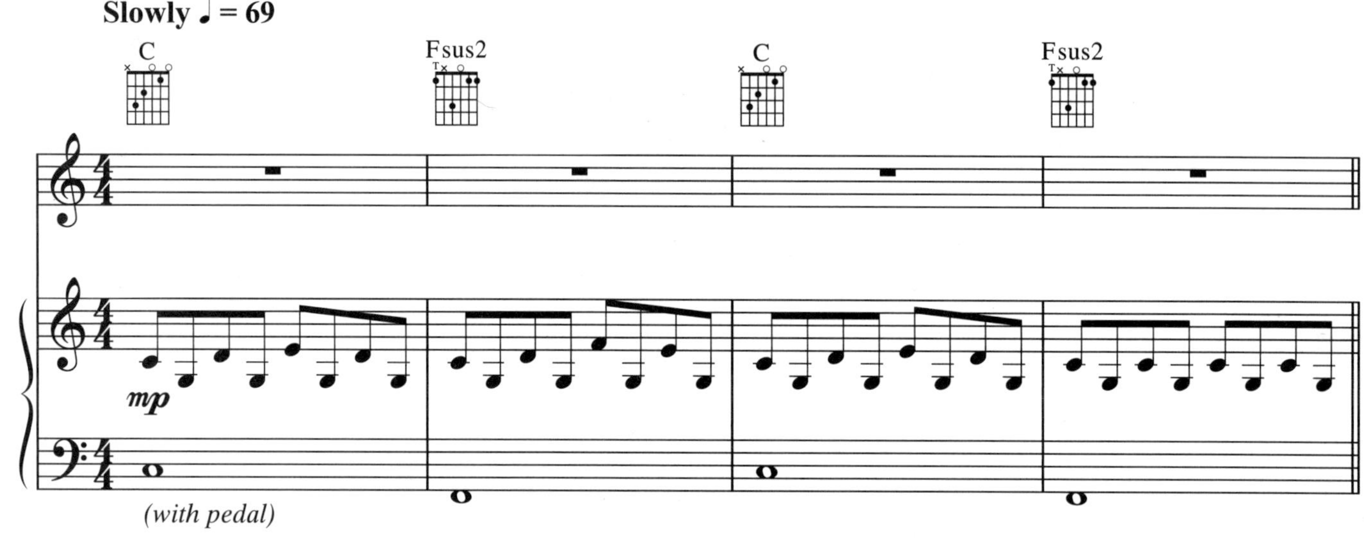
Slowly ♩ = 69
C
Fsus2
C
Fsus2
mp
(with pedal)

Verse 1:
C
Fsus2
C
Fsus2
1. I don't know you, but I want you all the more for that.

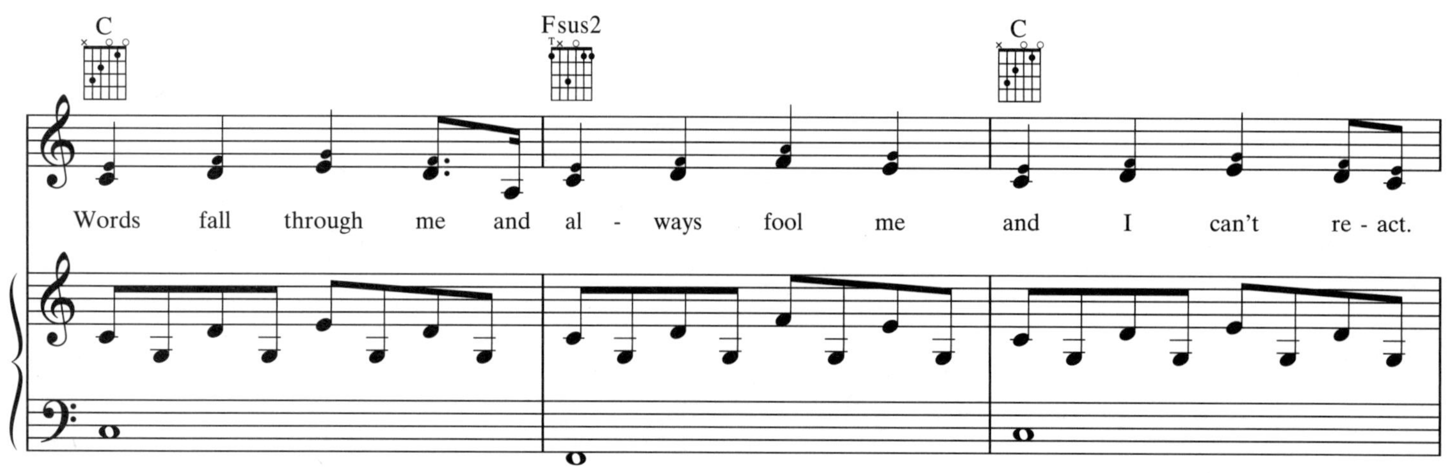
C
Fsus2
C
Words fall through me and al - ways fool me and I can't re - act.

Fsus2
Am7
G
Fsus2
G
Games that nev - er a - mount to more than they're
Am7
G
F(9)
Fsus2
meant will play them-selves out.
cresc.
Chorus:
C
Fsus2
Am7
Take this sink - in' boat and point it home, we've still got
mf
Fsus2
C
Fsus2
time.
Raise your hope - ful voice, you have a

Am7
Fsus2
choice, you make it now.
decresc.
Verse 2:
C
Fsus2
C
2. Fall - ing slow - ly, eyes that know me and I can't go back.
mp
Fsus2
C
Fsus2
C
Moods that take me and e - rase me and I'm paint - ed black.
Fsus2
Am
Em/G
Fsus2
G
Well, you have suf-fered e - nough and warred with your -

Am
Em/G
F(9)
Fsus2
self. It's time that you won.
cresc.
Chorus:
C
Fsus2
Am7
Take this sink - in' boat and point it home, we've still got
mf
Fsus2
C
Fsus2
time.
Raise your hope - ful voice, you have a
Am7
Fsus2
C
choice, you've made it now.
Fall - in' slow - ly,

Fsus2
Am7
Fsus2
sing your mel - o - dy, I'll sing it loud.
C
Fsus2
Am7
(Strings)
Fsus2
8va
G/F
Take it all.
Fsus2
I paid the cost too late,
now you're gone.

G/F
F(9)
(Strings)

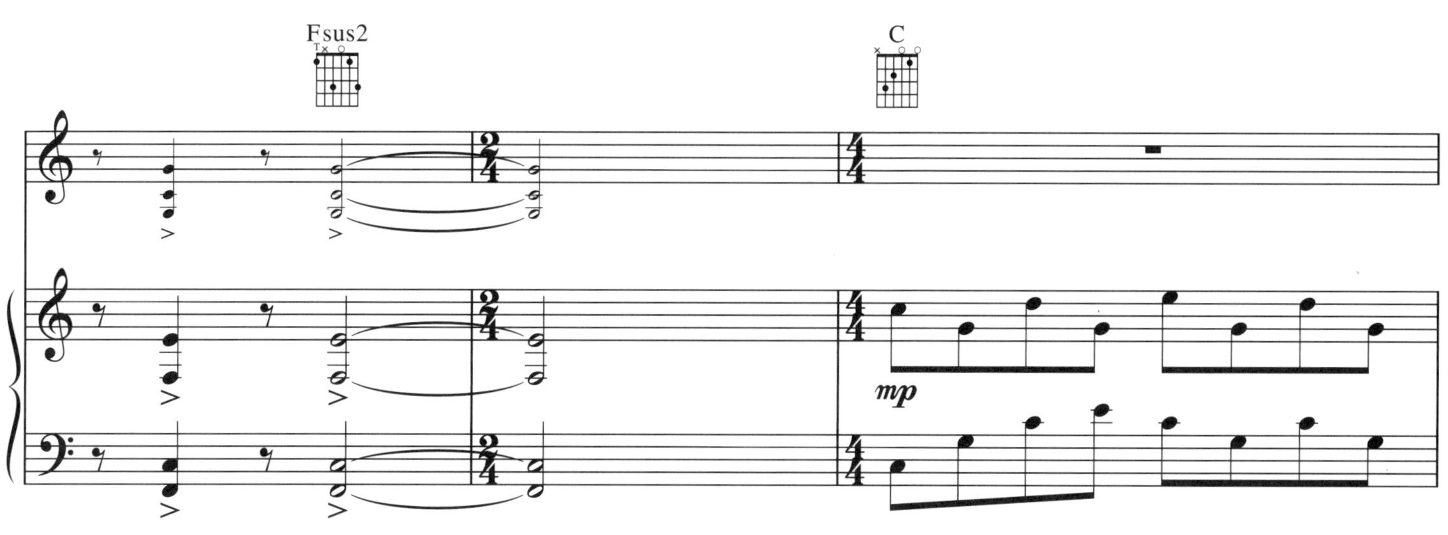
Fsus2
C
mp

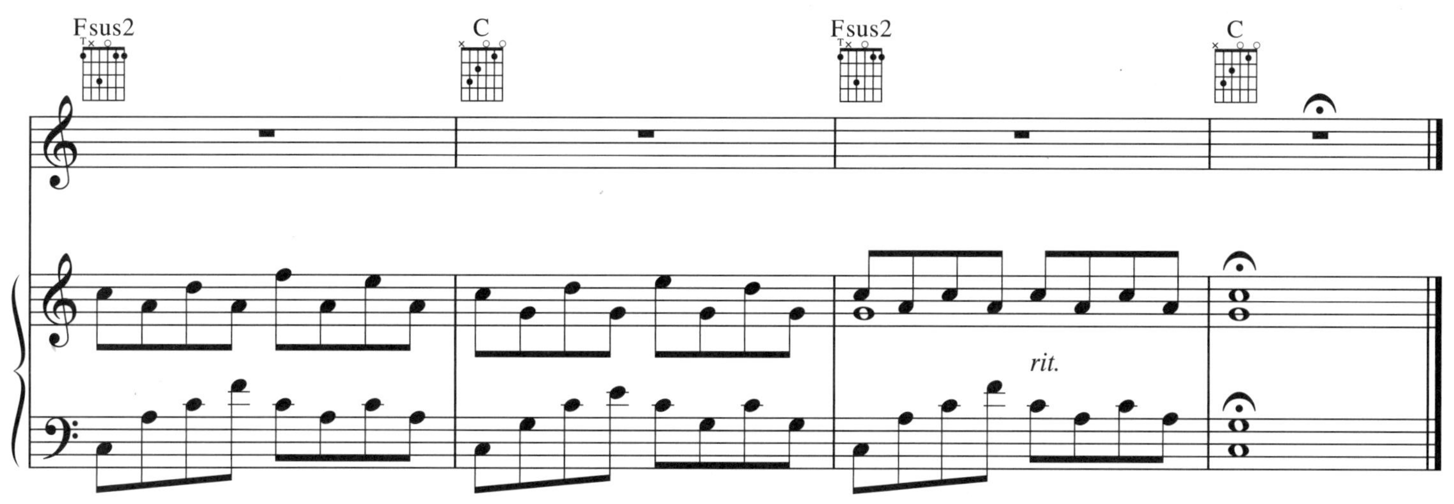
Fsus2
C
Fsus2
C
rit.

FOR WHAT IT'S WORTH

Words and Music by
STEPHEN STILLS

Moderately slow ♩ = 98
E
A
E
A
mf
Verses 1 & 2:
E
A
E
1. There's some - thing hap - pen - ing here, what it
2. There's bat - tle lines be - ing drawn. No - bod - y's
A
E
is ain't ex - act - ly clear. There's a
right if ev - 'ry - bod - y's wrong.
A
E
man with a gun o - ver there tell - in'
Young peo - ple speak - in' their minds, get - tin'

A
me I got to be - ware.
so much re - sis - tance from be - hind. I think it's time we
I think it's time we
Chorus:
E
D(9)
A
C
stop, chil - dren, what's that sound? Ev - 'ry - bod - y look what's go - in' down.
stop, hey, what's that sound? Ev - 'ry - bod - y look what's go - in' down.
1. E
A
E
A
2. E
A

E
A
Verses 3 & 4:
E A G E
3. What a field day for the heat; a thou - sand peo - ple in the
4. Par - a - noi - a strikes deep. In - to your life it will
A G E A G
street. Sing - in' songs and car - ry - in' signs,___ most - ly
creep. It starts when you're al - ways a - fraid.___ Step out of
E A G
say, "Hoo - ray for our side." It's time we
line, the man come and take you a - way. We bet - ter

Chorus:
E
D(9)
1.
A
C
stop, hey, what's that sound?
Ev - 'ry - bod - y look what's go - in' down.
stop, hey, what's that sound?
E
2.
A
C
Ev - 'ry - bod - y look what's go - in'. You bet - ter
Repeat ad lib. and fade
E
D(9)
A
C
stop. Hey, what's that sound?
Ev - 'ry - bod - y look what's go - in' down.

HEY THERE DELILAH

Words and Music by
TOM HIGGENSON

Moderately ♩ = 108
D5
F♯m
D5
F♯m
mp
Verses 1 & 2:
D5
F♯m
1. Hey there, De - li - lah, what's_ it like in New_ York Cit - y? I'm a thou -
2. Hey there, De - li - lah, I___ know times are get - ting hard, but just be - lieve_
D5
F♯m
Bm
Bm/A
sand miles a - way,_ but, girl,_ to - night__ you look so pret - ty, yes, you do.
___ me, girl, some - day__ I'll pay__ the bills__ with this gui - tar, we'll have it good.
G
A
Bm
A
A5
Times Square can't shine as bright as you.___ I swear it's true.
We'll have the life we knew we would._ My word is good.

D5 F♯m

Hey there, De-li - lah, don't_ you wor-ry a-bout the dis-tance, I'm_ right
Hey there, De-li - lah, I've_ got so_ much left to say._ If ev - 'ry

D5 F♯m Bm Bm/A

there. If you get lone-ly, give_ this song an-oth-er lis-ten. Close your eyes._
sim-ple song I wrote_to you_would take your breath a-way,_ I'd write it all._

G A Bm A A5

Lis-ten to my voice, it's my dis-guise._ I'm by your side.}
E-ven more in love_ with me,_ you'd fall. We'd have it all.}

𝄋 *Chorus:*

D5 D5/A Bm Bm/C♯ D5 D5/A

Oh, it's what you do to me,_ oh, it's what you do to me._

mf

Bm Bm/C♯ D5 D5/A Bm Bm/C♯
Oh, it's what you do to me,
To Coda
1.
D5 D5/A Bm Bm/C♯ D5 D5/A
oh, it's what you do to me. What you do to me.
2.
Bridge:
Bm Bm/A G
A thou - sand miles seems pret - ty far, but they've
A D5 D5/A Bm Bm/A
got planes and trains and cars. I'd walk to you if I had no oth-er way. Our

G A

friends would all make fun of us, and we'll just laugh a - long be - cause we know

D5 D5/C♯ Bm Bm/A G

that none of them have felt this way. De - li - lah, I can prom - ise you that by

A Bm

the time we get through, the world will nev - er, ev - er be the same,

A

and you're to blame.

Verse 3:
D5
F♯m
3. Hey there, De - li - lah, you be good__ and don't you miss__ me. Two more
Bm
Bm/A
years and you'll_ be done with school and I'll___ be mak-ing his - t'ry, like I do.
G
A
You know it's all be-cause of you.__
We can do what - ev - er we__ want_
G
__ to.________
Hey there, De - li - lah, here's to you.__
This one's for

D.S. 𝄋 al Coda
𝄌 Coda
A
A5
Bm
Bm/C♯
you.
What you do to me.
D5
D5/A
Oh,
whoa,
whoa.
whoa, whoa.
oh,
oh.

GOOD RIDDANCE

(Time of Your Life)

Lyrics by
BILLIE JOE

Music by
BILLIE JOE and GREEN DAY

Fast ♩ = 172
G5
C2
D5
mf
Verse:
1. An - oth - er turn - ing point, a fork stuck in the road.
2. So take the pho - to - graphs and still - frames in your mind.
3. (Inst. solo ad lib....
Time grabs you by the wrist, di - rects you where to go.
Hang it on a shelf in good health and good time.

Em D C(9) G

So make the best___ of___ this test___ and don't___ ask why.___
Tat - toos of mem - o - ries and dead___ skin___ on trial.___

Em D C(9) G

It's not a ques - tion, but___ a les - son___ learned_ in___ time.
For what it's worth,_ it___ was worth___ all___ the___ while.
...end solo)
It's

𝄋 *Chorus:*

Em G Em G

some - thing un - pre - dict - a - ble,___ but in the end___ it's right.___ I

Em D *To Coda* 𝄌 G

hope you had___ the time___ of___ your life.___

C2
D
G
1.2.
3.
D.S. 𝄋 al Coda
It's
Coda
G5
C2
D5
rit.

HIGH AND DRY

Words and Music by
THOMAS YORKE, JONATHAN GREENWOOD,
COLIN GREENWOOD, EDWARD O'BRIEN
and PHILIP SELWAY

Moderately slow ♩ = 86
F♯m7(4)
A(9)
mf
E
F♯m7(4)
A(9)
E
Verse:
F♯m7(4)
A(9)
1. Two jumps in a week, I bet you think that's pret-ty clev-er, don't
2. Dry - ing up in con - ver - sa - tion, you will be the one that can -

E
___ you, boy?
not talk.
F♯m7(4)
A(9)
Fly-ing on your mo-tor-cy-cle, watch-ing all the ground ___ be-neath ___
All your in-sides fall to piec-es, you just sit there wish-ing you could still ___
E
A/E
E
A/E
E
___ you drop.
___ make love.
You'd kill ___
F♯m7(4)
A(9)
___ your-self ___ for rec-og-ni-tion, kill your-self ___ to nev-er ev-
They're the ones ___ who'll hate ___ you when you think ___ you've got ___ the world ___ all ___

E Esus E

er stop. You broke
sussed out.

F♯m7(4) A(9)

an - oth - er mir - ror. You're turn - ing in - to some - thing you
They're the ones who spit at you. You will be the one scream -

E Esus E

are not.
ing out.

Don't leave me high,

Chorus:

F♯m7(4) A(9) E

don't leave me dry.

F♯m7(4)
1.
A(9)
Don't leave me high,
don't leave me dry.
E
F♯m7(4)
A(9)
E
2.
A(9)
E
don't leave me dry.

F♯m7(4)
A(9)
E
F♯m7(4)
A(9)
E
Oh, it's the best
Bridge:
F♯m7(4)
A(9)
thing that you've ev - er had, the best thing that you've ev - er, ev -
mp

E
er had.
It's the best
F♯m7(4)
thing that you've ev - er had,
A(9)
the best thing you have had has gone
E
a - way.
So don't leave me high,
cresc.
Chorus:
F♯m7(4)
A(9)
don't leave me
E
dry.

F♯m7(4)
A(9)
Don't leave me high,
don't leave me dry.
E
F♯m7(4)
Don't leave me high,
A(9)
E
don't leave me high,
F♯m7(4)
A(9)
E
don't leave me dry.

HOTEL CALIFORNIA

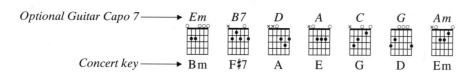

Optional Guitar Capo 7 →	*Em*	*B7*	*D*	*A*	*C*	*G*	*Am*
Concert key →	Bm	F♯7	A	E	G	D	Em

Words and Music by
DON HENLEY, GLENN FREY
and DON FELDER

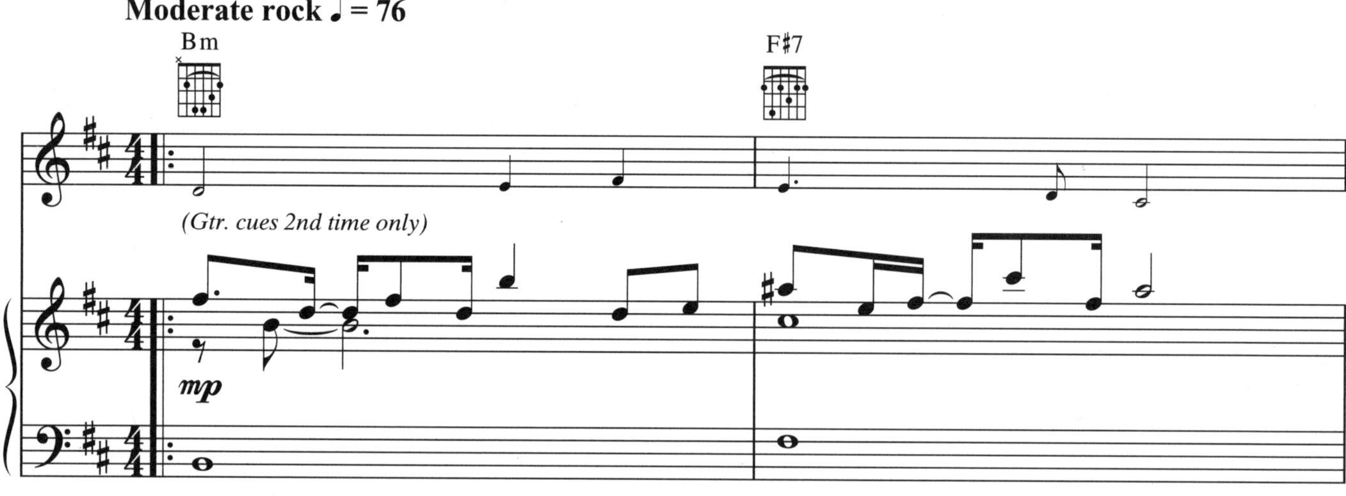
Moderate rock ♩ = 76
Bm
F♯7
(Gtr. cues 2nd time only)
mp

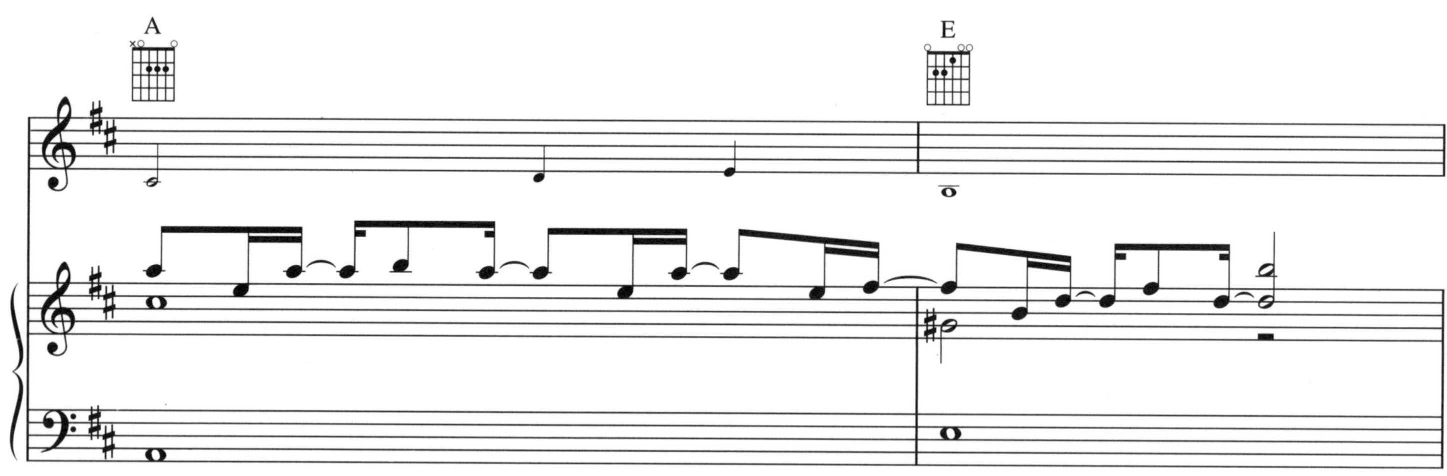
A
E

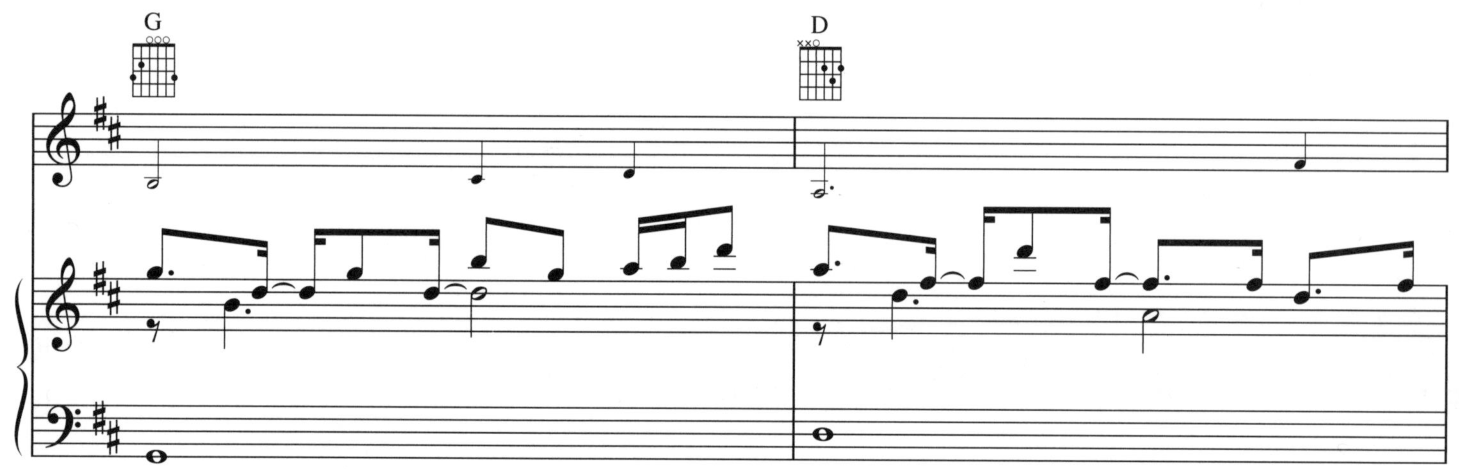
G
D

1.
2.
Em
F#7
F#7
Verses 1 & 2:
Bm
F#7
1. On a dark des-ert high-way,
cool wind in my hair,
2. Her mind is Tif - fa - ny twist - ed,
she got the Mer - ce - des bends.
mf
A
E
warm_smell of co-li - tas___
ris - ing up through the air.___
She got a lot of pret-ty, pret-ty boys_
that she calls friends.___
G
D
Up a - head in the dis - tance,
I saw a shim-mer - ing light.
How they dance in the court - yard,
sweet___ sum-mer sweat.

Em
F#7
My head grew heav - y and my sight grew dim,
I had to stop for the night.
Some dance to re-mem - ber,
some dance to for - get.
Bm
F#7
There she stood in the door - way,
I heard the mis - sion bell.
So I called up the cap - tain,
"Please bring me my wine."
He said,
A
E
And I was think - ing to my - self, "This could be heav - en or this could be hell."
"We have - n't had that spir - it here since nine - teen six - ty - nine.
G
D
Then she lit up a can - dle and she showed me the way.
And still those voic - es are call - ing from far a - way,

Em F♯7

There were voic - es down the cor - ri - dor,_ I thought I heard them say,_
wake you up in the mid - dle of the night just to hear them say,_

Chorus:

G D

"Wel-come_ to the Ho - tel Cal - i - for - nia! Such a

F♯7 Bm

love - ly place,_ (such a love - ly place,_) such a love - ly face._ They're

G D

Plen - ty of room_ at the Ho - tel Cal - i - for - nia, an - y
liv - in' it up__ at the Ho - tel Cal - i - for - nia. What a

1.
Em
F♯7
time_ of year_ (an - y time_ of year_) you can find_ it here._
nice_ sur - prise,_ (what a nice_ sur - prise,_) bring your
2.
F♯7
N.C.
al - i - bis._
Verse 3:
Bm
Mir - rors_ on the ceil - ing,_
mp
F♯7
the pink cham - pagne on ice,_ and she said,
A
"We are all just pris - on - ers here_
E
of our own_ de - vice."
G
And in the mas - ter's_ cham - bers,_

D
Em
they gath-ered for the feast.
They stab it with their steel-y knives, but they
F♯7
Bm
just can't kill the beast.
Last thing I re-mem-ber, I was
F♯7
A
run-ning for the door.
I had to find the pas-sage back to the
E
G
place I was be-fore.
"Re-lax," said the night-man. "We are

D
Em
pro - grammed_ to re - ceive.
You can check out an - y - time you like,
F#7
N.C.
3
but you can_ nev - er leave."_
Solo:
Bm
(Inst. solo ad lib....
(Cue notes 2nd time only)
F#7
A
E
G
D
Em

1.2.
F♯7
3.
F♯7
…end solo)
Bm
F♯7
A
E
G
D
Em
F♯7
Repeat and fade

A HORSE WITH NO NAME

Words and Music by
DEWEY BUNNELL

Moderately
Em
4 fr.
D9/6
Verse:
1. On the
mf
first part of the jour - ney I was look - ing at all the life,
nine days I let the horse run free 'cause the des - ert had turned to sea,
There were plants and birds and rocks and things, there were
There were plants and birds and rocks and things, there were
sand and hills and rings. The first thing I met was a
sand and hills and rings. The o - cean is a des - ert with it's

D9/6
4 fr.
Em
4 fr.
D9/6
4 fr.
fly with a buzz_ and the sky with no_ clouds,_ The
life un - der - ground and the per - fect dis - guise_ a - bove._ Un - der the
Em
4 fr.
D9/6
4 fr.
Em
4 fr.
heat was hot_ and the ground was dry,_ but the air was full_ of_ sound._
cit - ies_ lies a heart made of ground_ but the hu - mans will give_ no_ love._
D9/6
4 fr.
Em9
2 fr.
Dmaj9
I've
You see I've
been thru the des - ert on A Horse With No Name,_ it felt
f
Em9
2 fr.
Dmaj9
Em9
2 fr.
good to be out_ of the rain,_ In the des - ert_ you can re -

Dmaj9
Em9
2 fr.
To Coda
mem - ber your name 'cause there ain't no - one for to give you no pain.
La la la la la la la la la la la la
1.Dmaj9
2.Dmaj9
Verse:
Em
4 fr.
2. Af - ter two days in the
mf
D9/6
des - ert sun my skin be - gan to turn red, Af - ter

Em
4 fr.
D9/6
4 fr.
Em
4 fr.
three days in the des - ert fun I was look - ing at a riv - er bed.
D9/6
4 fr.
Em
4 fr.
D9/6
4 fr.
And the sto - ry it told of a riv - er that flowed made me
Em
4 fr.
D9/6
4 fr.
Chorus:
Em9
2 fr.
sad to think it was dead. You see I've been thru the des - ert on A
f
Dmaj9
Em9
2 fr.
Dmaj9
Horse With No Name, it felt good to be out of the rain, In the

Em9
2 fr.
Dmaj9
des - ert you can re - mem - ber your name 'cause there ain't no one for to
give you no pain. La la la la la la la la la la
la la la. La, 3. Af - ter
1.Dmaj9
2Dmaj9
D.S. al Coda
Coda
Repeat and fade
give you no pain. La, la la la la la la la la la la la la. La

JAR OF HEARTS

Words and Music by
DREW LAWRENCE, CHRISTINA PERRI
and BARRETT YERETSIAN

Slowly ♩ = 76
Verse 1:
Cm
E♭
1. I know I can't take one more step towards you,
mf
(with pedal)
B♭
Fm
Cm
'cause all that's wait - ing is re - gret.
And don't you know I'm not your
E♭
B♭
A♭
E♭/G
ghost an - y - more?
You lost the love I loved the most.

Fm
A♭
Cm
B♭
Fm
A♭
I learned to live half a-live, and now you want me one more time.
B♭sus
B♭
Chorus:
E♭
B♭
And who do you think you are? Run-ning 'round leav-ing
Cm
A♭
A♭m
scars, col-lect-ing your jar of hearts, and tear-ing love a-part.
E♭
B♭
You're gon-na catch a cold from the ice in-side your

Cm
A♭
A♭m
E♭
B♭/D
soul, so don't come back for me. Who do you think you are?
Verse 2:
Cm
E♭
B♭
2. I hear you're ask - ing all a - round if I am an - y - where to be
Fm
Cm
E♭
found. But I have grown too strong
B♭
A♭
E♭/G
Fm
A♭
to ev - er fall back in your arms. And I learned to live

Cm
B♭
Fm
A♭
B♭sus
B♭
half a - live,
and now you want me one more time.
Chorus:
E♭
B♭
And who do you think you are?
Run - ning 'round leav - ing
Cm
A♭
A♭m
scars, col - lect - ing your jar of hearts,
and tear - ing love a - part.
E♭
B♭
You're gon - na catch a cold
from the ice in - side your

Cm
To Coda
A♭
A♭m
E♭
soul, so don't come back for me. Who do you think you are? And
Bridge:
Cm
G/B
Cm7/B♭
F/A
Cm
G/B
it took so long just to feel al - right, re - mem - ber how to put back the
Cm7/B♭
F/A
Cm
G/B
Cm7/B♭
F/A
light in my eyes. I wish I had missed the first time that we kissed 'cause
Cm
G/B
Cm7/B♭
F/A
you broke all your prom - is - es. And

A♭
G
D.S. 𝄋 al Coda
now you're back, you don't get to get me back.
Coda
A♭
A♭m
E♭
me. Don't come back at all. And who do you think you are?
B♭
Cm
Run-ning 'round leav - ing scars, col - lect - ing your jar of hearts,
A♭
A♭m
E♭
and tear - ing love a - part. You're gon - na catch a cold

B♭
Cm
from the ice in - side your soul.
Don't come back for
A♭
A♭m
E♭
me.
Don't come back at all.
A♭dim7
E♭
A♭dim7
Who do you think you are?
Who do you think you
E♭
A♭dim7
E♭
are?
Who do you think you are?
rall.

KARMA POLICE

Words and Music by
THOMAS YORKE, JONATHAN GREENWOOD,
PHILIP SELWAY, COLIN GREENWOOD
and EDWARD O'BRIEN

Slowly ♩ = 76
Am
D9/F♯
Em
G
Am(9)
F
Em
G
mp
(with pedal)
Am(9)
D
G
D/F♯
C/E
Bm
Am
Bm
D
cresc.
Verse 1:
Am
D9/F♯
Em
G
Am(9)
F
1. Kar - ma po - lice, ar-rest this man, he talks in maths,
mf

Em
G
Am(9)
D
he buzz - es like a fridge, he's like a de -
G
D/F♯
C
Bm
Am
Bm
D
tuned ra - di - o.
Verses 2 & 3:
Am
D9/F♯
Em
G
Am(9)
F
2. Kar - ma po - lice, ar - rest this girl, her Hit - ler hair -
3. Kar - ma po - lice, I've giv - en all I can, it's not e - nough.
Em
G
Am(9)
D
do is mak - ing me feel ill and we have crashed
I've giv - en all I can, but we're still on

G
D/F♯
C
Bm
Am
Bm
D
her par - ty.
the pay - roll.
C
D/A
G
F♯7
C
D/A
mp
This is what you get,
this is what you get,
G
F♯7
C
D/A
G
Bm/F♯
this is what you get when you mess with us.
1.
C
Bm
D
cresc.
2.
C
Bm/F♯
D
cresc.

Chorus:
Bm
D
G
D
G
D
mf
For a min - ute there,
2. For a min - ute there,
I lost my - self,
I lost my - self.
E9
Bm
D
G
D
Phew, for a min - ute there,
I lost my - self,
1.
G
D
E9
Bm
D
I lost my - self.
G
D
G
D
E9

2.
G
D
E9
I lost my - self.
Bm
D
G
D
G
D
E9
Bm
D
G
D
G
D
E9
Bm

KNOCKING ON HEAVEN'S DOOR

Words and Music by
BOB DYLAN

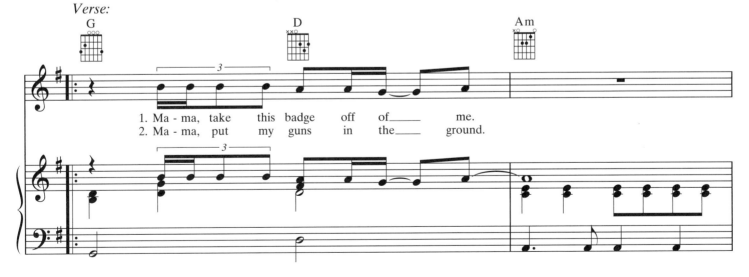

Moderately slow ♩ = 69
G
D
Am7
C
Ooh, ooh, ooh.
mp
Verse:
Am
1. Ma - ma, take this badge off of me.
2. Ma - ma, put my guns in the ground.
3

G
D
C
I can't use it an - y - more.
I can't shoot them an - y - more.
G
D
Am
It's get - tin' dark, too dark to see.
That long, black cloud is com - in' down.
G
D
C
Feel I'm knock - in' on Heav - en's door.
I feel I'm knock - in' on Heav - en's door.
Chorus:
G
D
Am
Knock, knock, knock - in' on Heav - en's door.
mf

G
D
C
Knock, knock, knock - in' on Heav - en's door.
G
D
Am
Knock, knock, knock - in' on Heav - en's door.
G
D
1. C
Knock, knock, knock - in' on Heav - en's door.
2. C
G
D
Am
Repeat and fade
Ooh, ooh, ooh.

KILLING ME SOFTLY WITH HIS SONG

Words and Music by
CHARLES FOX and NORMAN GIMBEL

Moderately ♩ = 120
Eb7sus
Eb7
mp
Verse:
Bbm7
Ab
Db
Fm
1. I heard he sang a good song, I heard he had a style.
2. I felt all flushed with fe - ver, em - bar-rassed by the crowd.
3. He sang as if he knew me, in all my dark de - spair.
And so I came to see him, to lis - ten for a while.
I felt he found my let - ters and read each one out loud.
And then he looked right through me, as if I was - n't there.

B♭m7
E♭7
A♭
C7
And there he was, this young boy, a strang - er to my eyes...
I prayed that he would fin - ish, but he just kept right on...
And he just kept on sing - ing, sing - ing clear and strong...
Chorus:
Fm
B♭m7
E♭
A♭
Strum-ming my pain with his fin - gers, sing-ing my life with his words.
Fm
B♭/D
E♭
D♭
Kill-ing me soft - ly with his song, kill-ing me soft - ly with his song, tell-ing my whole
To Coda
A♭
D♭
G♭maj7(♯11)
life with his words, kill-ing me soft - ly with his song.

1.2.
3.
Bridge:
F
Fm
Oh,
B♭m7
E♭
A♭
la la la la
B♭/D
E♭
D♭
A♭
la, oh, oh, la,
D♭
G♭maj7(♯11)
F
D.S. 𝄋 al Coda
la.

Coda
Gbmaj7(#11)
F
soft - ly.
He was
Chorus:
Fm7
Bbm7/F
Eb/Bb
Ab
strum-ming my pain,
yeah, he was sing - ing my life.
Fm
Bb/D
Eb
Db
Kill-ing me soft - ly with his song, kill-ing me soft - ly with his song, tell-ing my
Ab
Db
Gbmaj7(#11)
F
whole life with his words, kill-ing me soft - ly with his song.

LEAVING ON A JET PLANE

Words and Music by
JOHN DENVER

Moderately, with a light shuffle feel ♩ = 132
Amaj7/E
Bm7/E
D
mf
A
E
E7
1. All my
Verse:
Amaj7
D
Amaj7
bags are packed, I'm ready to go, I'm standing here out-
many times I've let you down, so many times I've
3. Now the time has come to leave you; one more time let

D
Amaj7
F♯m7
side your door, I hate to wake you up to say good-
played a - round, I tell you now, they don't mean a
me kiss you, then close your eyes, I'll be on my
E7
A
bye. But the dawn is break - in', it's
thing. Ev - 'ry place I go, I'll
way. Dream a - bout the
D
Amaj7
D
ear - ly morn, the tax - i's wait - in', he's blow - in' his horn. Al -
think of you, ev - 'ry song I sing, I'll sing for you, when
days to come, when I won't have to leave a - lone, a -
Amaj7
F♯m
E7
read - y I'm so lone - some I could die.
I come back, I'll {bring / wear} your wed - ding ring.
bout the times, I won't have to say:

Chorus:
A
D
So kiss me and smile for me,
A
D
A
Bm
tell me that you'll wait for me;
hold me like you'll nev - er let me
E7
A
D
go.
I'm a - leav - in' on a jet plane,
A
D/A
1. 2.
A
C♯m
I don't know when I'll be back a - gain;
oh, babe, I hate

3.
A
D
A
D/A
A
C♯m
Bm
E
to go.
2. There's so
leav - in'
on a jet plane,
I don't know when
I'll be back a - gain;
oh, babe,
I hate to
go.
dim.
p

LISTEN TO THE MUSIC

Words and Music by
TOM JOHNSTON

Moderately ♩ = 108
E
A/E
E
mf
A/E
E
A/E
E
A/E
E
Verses 1 & 2:
A/E
E
1. Don't you feel__ it grow - in' day__ by__ day?__
2. Well, I know__ you know bet - ter, ev - 'ry - thing__ I say.

B/D#
C#m
People gettin' ready for the news. Some are
Meet me in the country for a day. We'll be
B
A
happy, some are sad. Whoa,
happy and we'll dance. Oh,
E
A/E
E
we gotta let the music play.
we're gonna dance the blues away. And
What the people need is a way to make 'em smile. It
if I'm feelin' good to you, and you're feelin' good to me,

C♯m
ain't so hard to do if you know how. Got - ta get a
there ain't noth - in' we can do or say. Feel - in'
B
A
mes - sage, get it on through. Oh,
good, feel - in' fine. Oh,
E
now ma - ma's go'n' to af - ter 'while.
ba - by, let the mu - sic play.
Whoa,
Chorus:
C♯m7
A
whoa, lis - ten to the mu - sic. Whoa,

C♯m7
A
whoa,
lis - ten to the
mu - sic.
Whoa,
C♯m7
A
whoa,
lis - ten to the
mu - sic
all the time.
F♯7
A
1.
E
A/E
E

A/E
E
2.
Bridge:
E
D/E
Like a la - zy flow - in' riv - er
A/E
E
sur-round-ing cas - tles in the sky.
And the crowd is grow-in'
D/E
A/E
big-ger,
lis - t'nin' for the hap - py sounds, and I got to let them fly.
Whoa,

Chorus:
C♯m7
A
whoa, lis - ten to the mu - sic. Whoa,
C♯m7
A
whoa, lis - ten to the mu - sic. Whoa,
C♯m7
A
whoa, lis - ten to the mu - sic all the time.
F♯7
A
Repeat ad lib. and fade
Whoa,

LIGHTS

Words and Music by
NEAL SCHON and STEVE PERRY

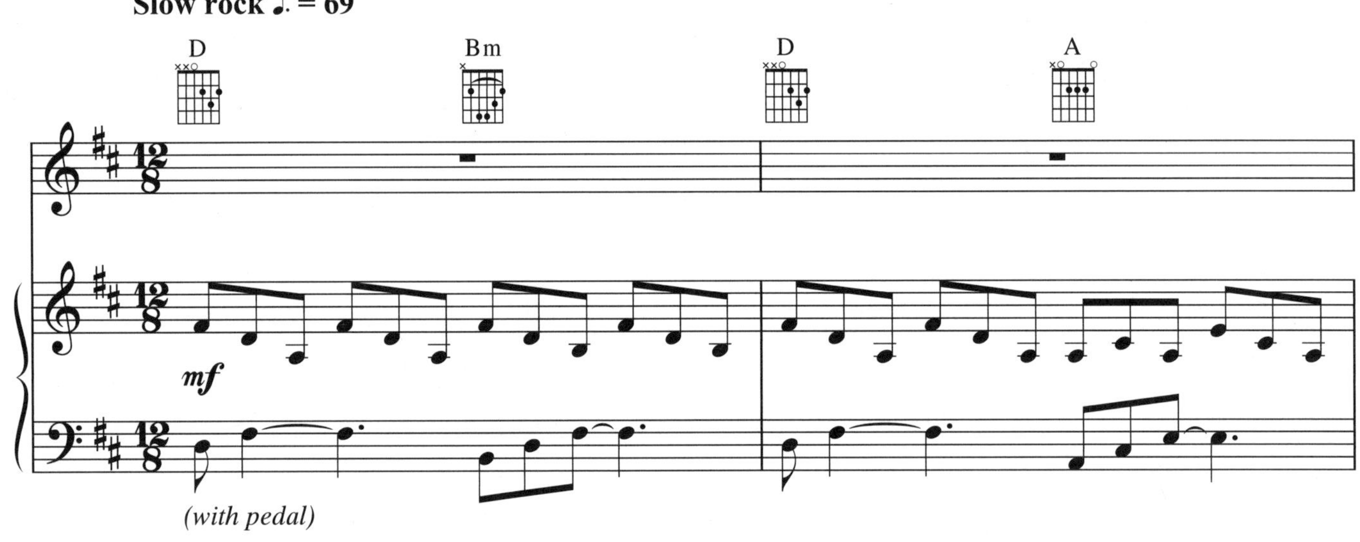
Slow rock ♩. = 69
D
Bm
D
A
mf
(with pedal)

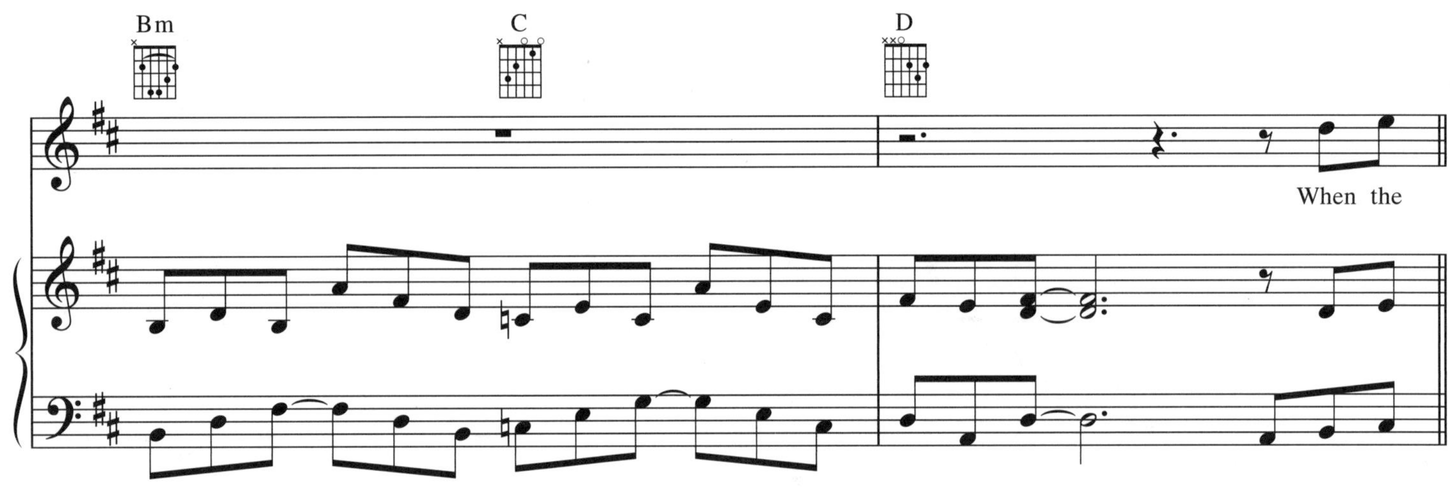
Bm
C
D
When the

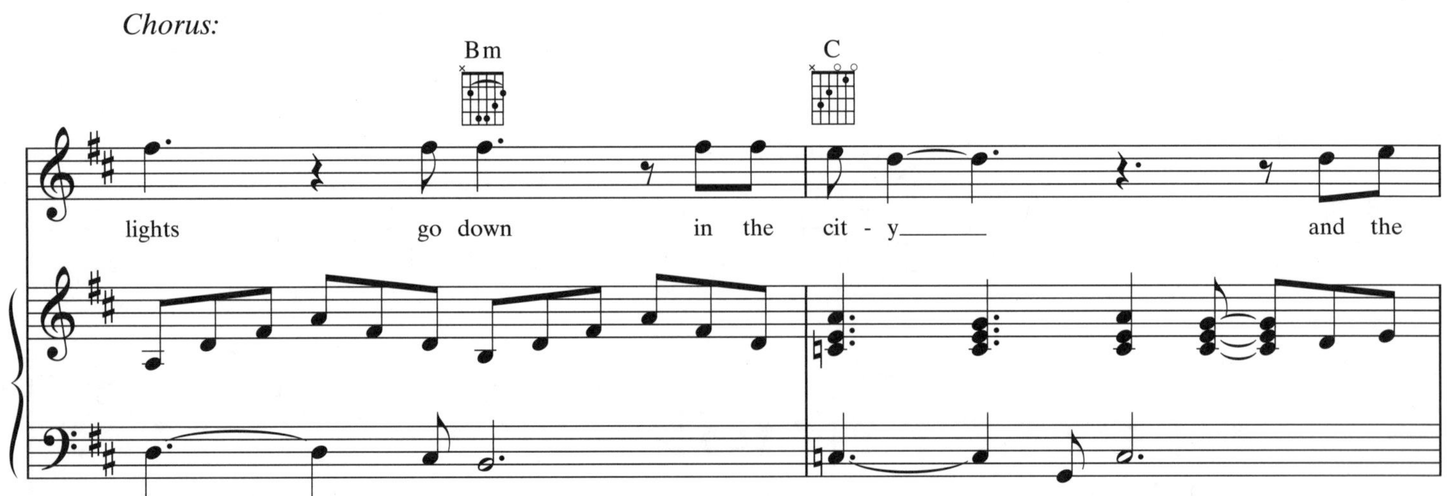
Chorus:
Bm
C
lights go down in the cit - y
and the

D
Bm
C
D/C
sun shines on the bay, ooh, I
want to be there in my city, oh.
Oh, oh, oh.
Verse:
1. So you think you're lonely?

D
Bm
C
Well, my friend, I'm lone - ly too.
D
Bm7
C
I want to get back to my cit - y by the bay - ee - ay.
Bm7
C
D
Oh, oh, oh. It's
Bridge:
Bm
A
G
D
sad, oh, there's been morn - ings out on the road with -
(2nd time - Guitar solo ad lib....
f

Bm A G D A F♯/A♯

out you, with - out your charms,

Bm A G D

oh, oh, my, my, my, my, my, my.

Bm7 C D

Oh, oh, oh.

...end solo) } When the

Chorus:

Bm7 C

lights go down in the cit - y and the

mf – f

D
Bm7
C
sun shines on the bay,
ooh, I
D
Bm7
C
want to be there in my city, oh.
Bm7
C
1.
D
Oh, ooh, oh,
oh.
Glissando
2.
D
Bm7
C
D
oh.
Oh, ooh, oh,
oh.
Mmm.

THE LOAD OUT

Words and Music by
JACKSON BROWNE
and BRYAN GAROFALO

Moderately ♩ = 104
G
G/B
C
mp
(with pedal)
Em
C
G/D
D/F♯
G
C/G
G
D5
G
Bm7
C
D
Em
C
G/D
D/F♯
G
C/G
G
D5
Now, the

G
G/B
C
D
seats are all emp - ty. Let the road - ies take the stage.
Em
C
D
G
Pack it up and tear it down. They're the
G/B
C
D
first to come and the last to leave, work - ing for that min - i - mum wage.
Em
C
D
G
C
They'll set it up in an - oth - er town.

G
Em
E♭dim7
To - night the peo - ple were so fine.
C
C♯dim7
G/D
They wait - ed there in line. And when they got up on their feet,
Em
D/F♯
C/G
they made the show. And that was
G
G/B
C
D
sweet. But I can hear the sound of slam-ming doors and fold - ing chairs,

Em C D G C/G G D
and that's a sound_ they'll nev - er know._
G C G
Now, roll them cas - es out and lift them amps._ And haul them truss - es down and
C G G/B
get 'em up them ramps 'cause when it comes to mov - ing me,___ you know_
C D G
___ you guys___ are the champs._ But when that last gui - tar's___ been packed_

G/B
C
D
Em
a - way, you know that I still want to play. So just make
C
D
Em
D/F♯
sure you've got it all set to go be-fore you come for my pi - an - o.
Guitar solo:
G
G/B
C
Em
(solo with bottleneck)
mf
C
D
G
C/G
G
D
G
G/B

C
D
Em
C
D
G
C/G
G
But the
mp
Em
E♭dim7
C
C♯dim7
band's on the bus and they're wait - ing to go.
We got to
G/D
Em
D/F♯
C/G
drive all night and do the show in Chi - ca - go
G
G/B
or De - troit.
I don't know.
We do so

C
D
Em
C
D
many - y shows in a row.
And these towns all look the same.
G
G/B
We just pass the time in the ho - tel rooms and
C
D
Em
C
wan - der 'round back - stage 'til those lights come up and we hear
D
that crowd and we re - mem - ber why we came.
cresc.

Synth. solo:
G
G/B
C
D
Em
(solo sounds 8va higher)
C
D
G
C
G
D
G
G/B
C
D
Em
C
D
G
C
G
D
Now, we got

G
Em
coun - try and west - ern on the bus;
R. and B.
C
We got dis - co in eight-tracks and cas-settes in ster - e - o.
G
D
G
And we got ru - ral scenes and mag -
G/B
C
D
Em
a - zines and we got truck-ers on C. B.
And we got Rich-ard
mf

C D G
Pry-or on the vid-e-o. We've got time to think of the
G/B C D Em
ones we love while the miles roll a-way. But the
C D
on-ly time that seems too short is the time that we get to play.
G C
Peo-ple, you've got the pow-er o-ver what we do. You can

G
C
G
sit there and wait or you can pull us through. Come a - long. Sing the
G/B
C
D
G
song. You know that you can't go wrong. 'Cause when that morn-ing sun comes
dim.
G/B
C
D
Em
beat - ing down, you're gon-na wake up in your town. But
mp
C
D
Em
D/F♯
we'll be sched-uled to ap-pear a thou - sand miles a - way from here.

LOSING MY RELIGION

Words and Music by
WILLIAM BERRY, PETER BUCK,
MICHAEL MILLS and MICHAEL STIPE

Moderately Fast
no chord

F F6/9 F Dm G Am

mf

F F6/9 F Dm G Am G

Am

Oh, ____________ life _____ is big - ger.
- per of ev - ery wak - ing hour, _

Em Am

It's big - ger __ than you __ and you __ are not ___ me. The
__ I'm choos - ing my con - fes - sions

Em
lengths that I will go to, the dis - tance in your eyes.
try - ing to keep an eye on you like a hurt,
Am
Em
lost and blind - ed fool, fool.
Oh no, I've
Oh no, I've
Dm
said too much.
said too much.
I set it up.
I set it up.
G
Am
1.,3. That's me in the cor - ner.
2. Con - sid - er this, con -

Em
That's me in the spot - light los - ing my re - lig -
sid - er this the hint of the cen - tu - ry. Con - sid - er this
Am
Em
ion try - ing to keep up with you
the slip that brought me to my knees
Am
and I don't know if I can do it.
failed. What if all these fan-ta - sies come
Em
Dm
Oh no, I've said too much. I
flail - ing a - round? And now, I've said

G
have - n't said e - nough.
too much.
I thought that I heard you laugh -
F
G
Am
ing. I thought that I heard you sing.
F
Dm7
G
To Coda
I think I thought I saw you try.
Am
G
1
2
Ev - er - y whis -

Am
Am/G
Fmaj7
Am/G
C
Dm
But that was just a dream.
C
Dm
D.S. al Coda
That was just a dream. That's me in the cor-
CODA
Am
F
Dm7
G
Am
But that was just a dream.
Try.

F
Cry.
Why?
Try.
That was just a dream,
Dm7
G
Am
G
just a dream,
just a dream,
dream.
Am
1
2
rit.

THE LUCKIEST

Words and Music by
BEN FOLDS
Con sentimento ♩ = 60
Intro:
D
G
D
A
Bm7
F♯m
G
A7
poco rit.
Verse:
D
A
D
G
a tempo
1. I don't get man-y things right the first time. In
I'd been born fif - ty years be - fore you in a house
door there's an old man who lived in - to his nine - ties and one day

D
Bm
C
fact, I am told that a lot. Now I know
on the street where you live? May-be I'd
passed a-way in his sleep. And his wife,
A
A7/C♯
D
G
all the wrong turns, the stum-bles and falls brought me here.
be out-side as you passed on your bike, would I know?
she stayed for a cou-ple of days and passed a-way.
D
Bm
F♯m
A
Bm
G
Bm
E7
3rd time
And where was I be-fore the day that I first saw your love-ly face?
In a wide sea of eyes see one pair that I
I'm sor-ry I know that's a strange way to tell you that I know

A
F♯m
G
Now I see it ev-'ry day and I
rec-og-nize and I
we be-long, that I
Chorus:
D/A
A7
D
A
know that I am,
Bm
F♯m
G
D/A
A7
To Coda
I am, I am the
D
A7
1.
D
G
D
A7
luck-i-est.
2. What if

2.
Em7
Bm
A7
I love you more than I have ev-er found a way to say
D
G
D/A
A7
D.S. 𝄋 al Coda
to you.
3. Next
Coda
Bm
F♯m
G
Asus
A7
D
luck-i-est.
poco rit.
8vb

MAGGIE MAY

Words and Music by
ROD STEWART and MARTIN QUITTENTON

Moderately fast ♩ = 132
D
Em
G
D
Dsus2 sus4
mf
D
Em
G
D
Em
F♯m
Verse:
A
G
D
1. Wake up, Mag-gie, I think I got some-thin' to say to you.__ It's
2. 3. 4. See additional lyrics
A
G
D
late Sep - tem-ber and I real - ly should_ be back___ at__ school. I

G
D
G
A
know I keep you a - mused, but I feel I'm be - ing used. Oh,
Em
F♯m
Em7
Asus/E
Mag - gie, I could - n't have tried an - y more. You
Em
A
Em
led me a - way from home, just to save you from be - in' a -
A
Em
A
lone. You stole my heart and that's what real - ly hurts.

D

1.2. 3.4.

2. The

Em7 A D G

1. G A D D.S. 𝄋

Em7

2. G A D 3. G A

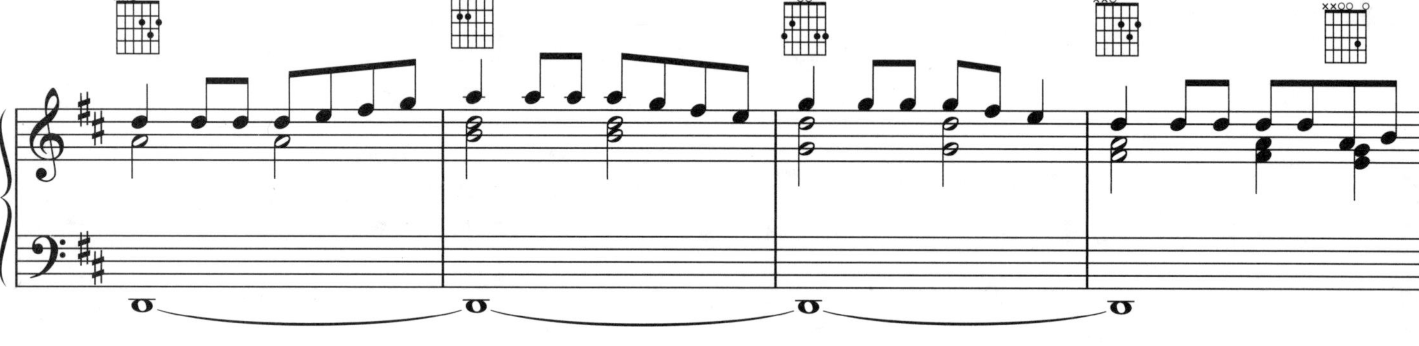
D
Em
G
D
Dsus2 sus4

D
Em
G
1.–3.
Dsus2 sus4
4.
1. Mag-gie, I wish I'd nev - er seen your face.
(2.) get on back home one of these days.
3. 4. (etc.) Instr. repeat ad lib. and fade
Repeat ad lib. and fade
2. I'll

Verse 2:
The morning sun, when it's in your face, really shows your age.
But that don't worry me none; in my eyes you're ev'rything.
I laughed at all of your jokes; my love you didn't need to coax.
Oh, Maggie, I couldn't have tried any more.
You led me away home, just to save you from being alone.
You stole my soul, and that's a pain I can do without.

Verse 3:
All I needed was a friend to lend a guiding hand.
But you turned into a lover, and, Mother, what a lover! You wore me out.
All you did was wreck my bed, and in the morning kick me in the head.
Oh, Maggie, I couldn't have tried any more.
You led me away home, 'cause you didn't want to be alone.
You stole my heart; I couldn't leave you if I tried.

Verse 4:
I suppose I could collect my books and get on back to school,
Or steal my Daddy's cue and make a living out of playin' pool,
Or find myself a rock 'n' roll band that needs a helpin' hand.
Oh, Maggie, I wish I'd never seen your face.
You made a first-class fool out of me, but I'm as blind as a fool can be.
You stole my heart, but I love you anyway.

MAKE YOU FEEL MY LOVE

Words and Music by
BOB DYLAN
Slowly ♩ = 76
B♭
F/A
A♭
E♭
mf
(with pedal)
E♭m
B♭
C7
E♭/F
B♭
Verses 1 & 2:
F/A
1. When the rain__ is blow - ing__ in your face,__
2. When the eve - ning__ shad - ows and the__ stars ap - pear__
A♭
E♭
and the whole_ world is on____ your case,__
and there is no___ one there to dry____ your tears,__________

E♭m
B♭
I could of - fer you a warm em - brace
I could hold you for a mil - lion years
C7
E♭/F
1.
B♭
2.
B♭
to make you feel my love.
to make you feel my love.
Bridge:
E♭
B♭/F
1. I know you have - n't made your mind up yet,
2. The storms are rag - ing on the roll - ing sea
G♭+
E♭/G
B♭
but I would nev - er do you wrong.
and on the high - way of re - gret.

E♭
B♭
I've known it from the moment that we___ met.___
The winds of change are blow - ing wild___ and free.___
C7*
F
No doubt in my mind where you be - long.___
You ain't___ seen noth - ing like me yet.___
Verses 3 & 4:
B♭
F/A
3. I'd go hun - gry, I'd___ go___ black and blue,___
4. I could make you hap - py, make_ your_ dreams come true,___
A♭
E♭
E♭m
I'd go crawl - ing down the av - e - nue.__
noth - ing that I would - n't do.___
Know there's noth - ing_ that_ I___
Go to the ends of_ the

*Play Cm7 2nd time.

To Coda 𝄌

B♭ C7 E♭/F B♭

would - n't do___ to make you feel my love.___

earth for you___ to make you feel my love,_

B♭ F/A A♭ E♭

E♭m B♭ C7 E♭/F B♭

D.S. 𝄋 al Coda

𝄌 *Coda*

B♭ C7 E♭/F B♭

___ to make you feel my love.___

dim.

rit.

MARGARITAVILLE

Words and Music by
JIMMY BUFFETT

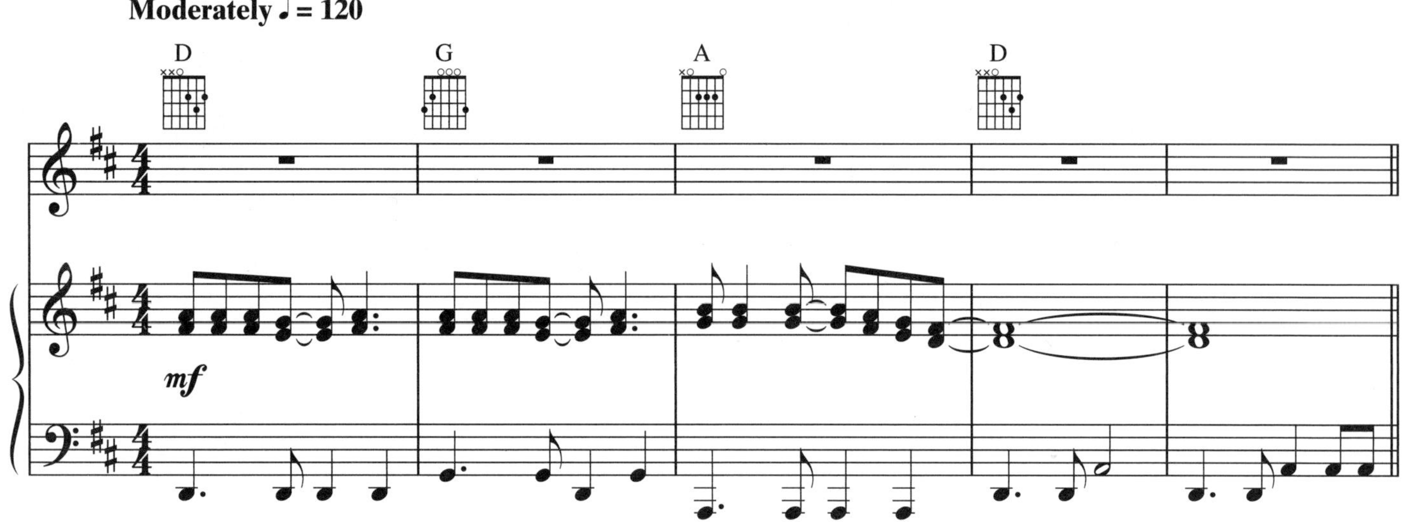
Moderately ♩ = 120
D
G
A
D
mf

Verse:
D
1. Nib - blin' on sponge - cake, watch - in' the sun
2. Don't know the rea - son I stayed here all sea -
3. I blew out my flip - flop, stepped on a pop -

bake; all of those tour - ists cov - ered with oil.
son with noth - ing to show but this brand - new tat - too.
top; cut my heel, had to cruise on back home.

A
Strum-min' my six - string
But it's a real beau - ty,
But there's booze in the blend - er,
on my front porch swing.
a Mex - i - can cu - tie,
and soon it will ren - der
Smell those shrimp;
how it got
that fro - zen con -
D
they're be - gin - ning to boil.
here I have - n't a clue.
coc - tion that helps me hang on.
Chorus:
G
A
D
D7
Wast-in' a - way a - gain in Mar - ga - ri - ta - ville,

G
A
D
search - in' for my lost shak - er of salt.
D7
G
A
Some people claim that there's a
D
A/C♯
G
A
wom - an to blame,
but I know
now I think,
but I know
1.2.
D
it's no - bod - y's fault.
hell, it could be my fault.
it's my own damn fault.

3.
D
G
Yes, and some_ peo - ple claim_
A
D
A/C♯
G
_ that there's_ a wom - an to blame,_ and I know_
A
D
it's my own_ damn_ fault._
G
A
D

MARRY ME

Words and Music by
SAM HOLLANDER
and PAT MONAHAN

Moderately 𝅗𝅥 = 88

C/E F2

mp

(with pedal)

C/E F2

Verse:

C Gsus/B G/B

1. For - ev - er could nev - er be long e - nough_ for me to
2. To - geth - er can nev - er be close e - nough_ for me to

Am7 Gsus F2

feel like I've had long e - nough_ with you.
feel like I am close e - nough_ to you.

C
Gsus/B
G/B
For - get the world, now, we won't let them see.
You wear white and I'll wear out the words "I love
Am7
Gsus
F2
But there's one thing left to do.
you" and "you're beau-ti - ful."
C/E
F2
Now that the weight has lift - ed
Now that the wait is o - ver
C/E
F2
and love has sure - ly shift - ed my way,
and love has fi - n'lly showed her my way,

Chorus:
C
Gsus/B
G/B
Am7
mar - ry me to-day
Gsus
F2
C
and ev - 'ry day.
Mar - ry
Gsus/B
G/B
Am7
Gsus
F2
me.
If I ev - er get the nerve to say "hel - lo" in this ca -
C/E
F2
fé, say you will.
Mm,
say you will,

C/E
To Coda
F2
1.
2.
mm.
Bridge:
B♭2
F(9)/A
Prom - ise me you'll al - ways be
C
Gsus/B
G/B
hap - py by my side.
B♭2
F(9)/A
I prom - ise to sing to you

C
Gsus/B
G/B
when all the mu - sic dies.
B♭2
F(9)/A
D.S. 𝄋 al Coda
And
Coda
F2
mm,
mar - ry
C/E
F2
me,
mm.

MOONDANCE

Words and Music by
VAN MORRISON

Jazz shuffle ♩ = 132
Am7 Bm7 Am7 Bm7 Am7 Bm7 Am7 Bm7
1. Well, it's a
mf
Verse:
Am7 Bm7 Am7 Bm7 Am7 Bm7
(3.) mar - vel - ous night for a moon - dance with the stars up a - bove in your eyes,
(2.) wan - na make love to you to - night, I can't wait 'til the morn - ing has come.
Am7 Bm7 Am7 Bm7 Am7 Bm7
a fan - tab - u - lous night to make ro - mance 'neath the
And I know now the time is just right and straight

Am7
Bm7
cov - er of Oc - to - ber skies.
in - to my arms_ you will run.
And all the leaves on the trees are fall - ing to the
And when you come, my heart will be wait - ing to make
sound of the breez - es that blow.
sure that you're nev - er a - lone.
And I'm try - ing to please_ to the call -
There and then, all my dreams_ will come true,_
ing of your heart - strings that play soft and low.
_ dear, there and then, will I make you my own.
And all the
And ev - 'ry
Dm6
night's_ mag - ic seems to whis - per and hush,
time I_ touch_ you, you just trem - ble in - side.
and all the
And I know

Dm6 Am7 N.C. Dm6 N.C. E7(♯5) Am7
soft moon - light seems to shine in your blush.
how much you want me; that, you can't hide.
Can I
Chorus:
Dm7 Am7 Dm7 Am7 Dm7 Am7
just have one more moon - dance with you, my love?
Dm7 Am7 Dm7 Am7 Dm7 Am7
Can I just make some more ro - mance with you,
To Coda
Dm7 Am7
1. E7
2. E7
my love?
2. Well, I

Piano solo:
Am7
Bm7
(play straight 8th notes)
8va
(8va)
3
5

Am7
Bm7
Am7
Bm7
Am7
Bm7
Saxophone solo:
Am7
Dm6
Am7
Dm6
Am7
Dm6
Am7
N.C.
Dm6
N.C.
E 7(♯5)
Am7

Dm7
Am7
Dm7
Am7
Dm7
Am7
Dm7
Am7
Dm7
Am7
Dm7
Am7
Dm7
Am7
E7
D.S. 𝄋 al Coda
𝄌 Coda
E7
3. Well, it's a
One more moon -
Am7
Bm7
Am7
Bm7
Am7
Bm7
Am7
Bm7
dance with you in the moon-light, on a

Am7
Bm7
mag - ic night.
La la la
Am7
Bm7
la, in the moon - light,
on a
Am7
Bm7
mag - ic night.
Am
Em/G
Can't I just have one
Fmaj7
Em7
Dm7
N.C.
Am9
more moon - dance with you, my love?

MY IMMORTAL

Words and Music by
BEN MOODY, AMY LEE
and DAVID HODGES

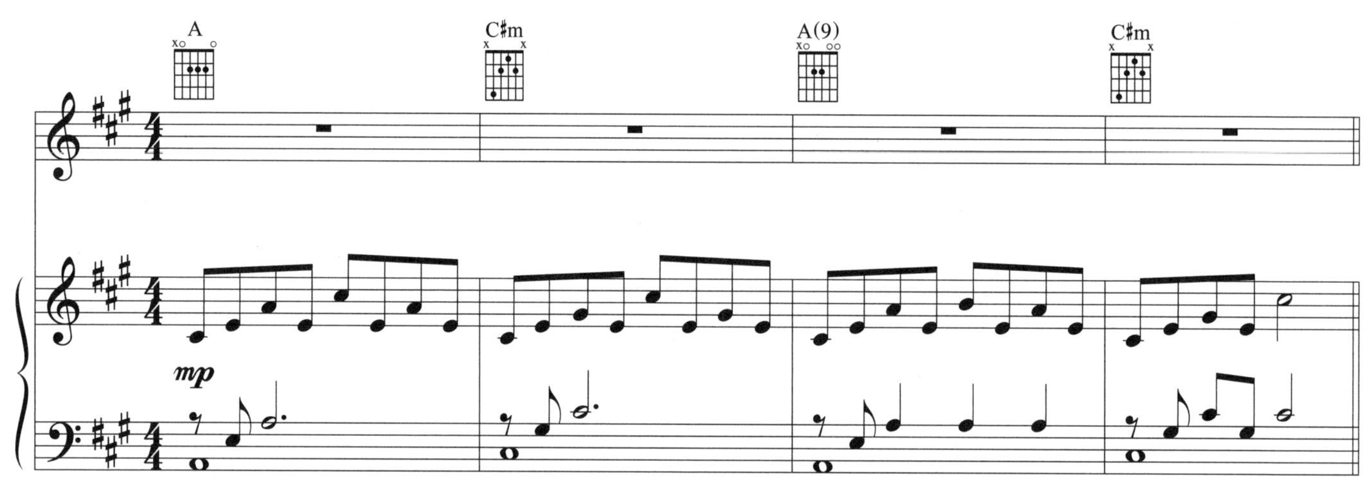
Slowly and freely ♩ = 80
A
C♯m
A(9)
C♯m
mp

Verse:
A
C♯m
A(9)
1. I'm so tired of be - ing here,
2. See additional lyrics
sup - pressed by all my

C♯m
A
child - ish fears.
And if you have to leave,

C♯m
A(9)
I wish that you would just leave, 'cause your presence still lingers here,
C♯m
F♯m
C♯m
4fr.
and it won't leave me a - lone. These wounds won't seem to heal.
F♯m
C♯m
F♯m
C♯m
E
Esus
E
This pain is just too real. There's just too much that time can - not e - rase.
Chorus:
F♯m
E/D
Esus/D
E
C♯m
When you cried, I'd wipe a - way all of your tears.

F♯m
E/D
Esus/D
E
C♯m
4fr.
When you'd scream, I'd fight a - way all of your fears.
And I've held your hand through all of these years, but you still
have all of me.
To Coda
1.
A
A(9)

Bridge:
2.
D(9)
F♯m
C♯m
4fr.
all of me.
I've tried so hard to tell my - self that you're
D
Bm9
C♯m
4fr.
gone. And though you're still with me,
E/D
D
E
Esus
F♯m
D
I've been a - lone all a - long.
D.S. 𝄋 al Coda
E
C♯m
4fr.
F♯m
D
E
C♯m
4fr.

Coda
A
C♯m
all of me, all of
A(9)
C♯m
A
me, all,
C♯m
A(9)
C♯m
A
me.

Verse 2:
You used to captivate me
By your resonating light.
But, now I'm bound by the life you left behind.
Your face, it haunts
My once pleasant dreams.
Your voice, it chased away
All the sanity in me.
These wounds won't seem to heal.
This pain is just too real.
There's just too much that time can not erase.
(To Chorus:)

NEED YOU NOW

Words and Music by
DAVE HAYWOOD, CHARLES KELLEY,
HILLARY SCOTT and JOSH KEAR

Moderately ♩ = 108
Guitar Capo 4 → Fmaj9
Piano → Amaj9
Am
C♯m
mp
Fmaj9
Amaj9
mf
Am
C♯m
Verse 1 (sing 1st time only):
Fmaj9
Female: Amaj9
1. Pic - ture - per - fect mem - 'ries, scat-tered all a - round the floor._
(Male:) Verse 2 (sing 2nd time only):
oth - er shot of whis - key, can't stop look - ing at the door,_

*Alternate between open G and A on the 3rd string.

Am
C♯m
Fmaj9
Amaj9
Reach - ing for the phone, 'cause
wish - ing you'd come sweep - ing in
I can't fight it an - y - more.
the way you did be - fore.
Both:
And I won -
der if I ev - er cross your mind.

Fmaj9
Amaj9

For me it hap - pens all___ the time.___ It's a

For me it hap - pens all_______ the time.___ It's a

Chorus:

C
E
Em
G♯m

Both:

quar-ter af - ter one, I'm___ all a - lone and I need__ you__ now._______ }
quar-ter af - ter one, I'm___ a lit - tle drunk and I need__ you__ now._______ }

C
E

I said___ I would-n't call, but I lost___ all con - trol and I need_

Em
G♯m
Fmaj9
Amaj9

___ you__ now._______ And I don't__ know how__ I can do_

1.
with - out.
I just need you now.
Am
C♯m
Male:
2. An -
2.
Am
C♯m
G/B
B/D♯
C
E
just need you now.
(Inst. solo ad lib....
Fmaj9
Amaj9
Gsus
Bsus
Am
C♯m
G/B
B/D♯
C
E
Male:
Whoa, whoa.

Fmaj9
Amaj9
Gsus
Bsus
Both:
...end solo) Guess I'd rath -
Fmaj9
Amaj9
Am
C♯m
er hurt than feel nothing at all.
Chorus:
Gsus
Bsus
C
E
Female:
It's a quarter after one, I'm all alone and I need
you now.
Em
G♯m
C
E
Male:
And I said I would-n't call, but
mp
mf

Em
G♯m
Both:
I'm a lit - tle drunk and I need__ you__ now.______
And I don't_
Fmaj9
Amaj9
___ know how__ I can do_____ with - out.______
I______ just need__ you now._
C
E
Em
G♯m
I__
C
E
___ just need__ you now.

Em
G♯m
C
E
Em
G♯m
Female:
Oh, ba - by, I need you now.
C
E
Em
G♯m
C
E
mp

THE NIGHT THEY DROVE OLD DIXIE DOWN

Words and Music by
ROBBIE ROBERTSON

Moderately ♩ = 120
C
mf
Verse:
Am
C
F
1. Vir - gil Caine is my name, and I drove on the Dan - ville train,
2.3. See additional lyrics
Am
C
Am
'til so much cav - al - ry came and

*Recording in D flat major.

F Am F

tore up the tracks a - gain.___ In the win - ter of

C Am Fm

'Six - ty - five, we were hun - gry,___ just___ bare - ly a - live.___

Am F C

I took the train to Rich - mond that fell; it was a time I re -

A D7

mem - ber, oh,___ so___ well.___ The night_

Chorus:
C
Am
F
C
they drove old Dix - ie down. And all the
Am
C
Am
F
bells were ring - in' the night they drove old Dix - ie down.
C
Am
C
And all the peo - ple were sing - in'. They went: La la la
Am
D7
F
la la la, la la la la la la la la la.

1.2.
C
3.
Am

Verse 2:
Back with my wife in Tennessee,
And one day she said to me,
"Virgil, quick come see.
There goes the Robert E. Lee."
Now, I don't mind I'm choppin' wood,
And I don't care if my money's no good.
Just take what you need and leave the rest,
But they should never have taken the very best.
(To Chorus:)

Verse 3:
Like my father before me,
I'm a working man.
And like my brother before me,
I took a rebel stand.
Well, he was just eighteen, proud and brave,
But a Yankee laid him in his grave.
I swear by the blood below my feet,
You can't raise the Caine back up
When it's in defeat.
(To Chorus:)

NIGHTSWIMMING

Words and Music by
WILLIAM BERRY, PETER BUCK,
MICHAEL MILLS and MICHAEL STIPE

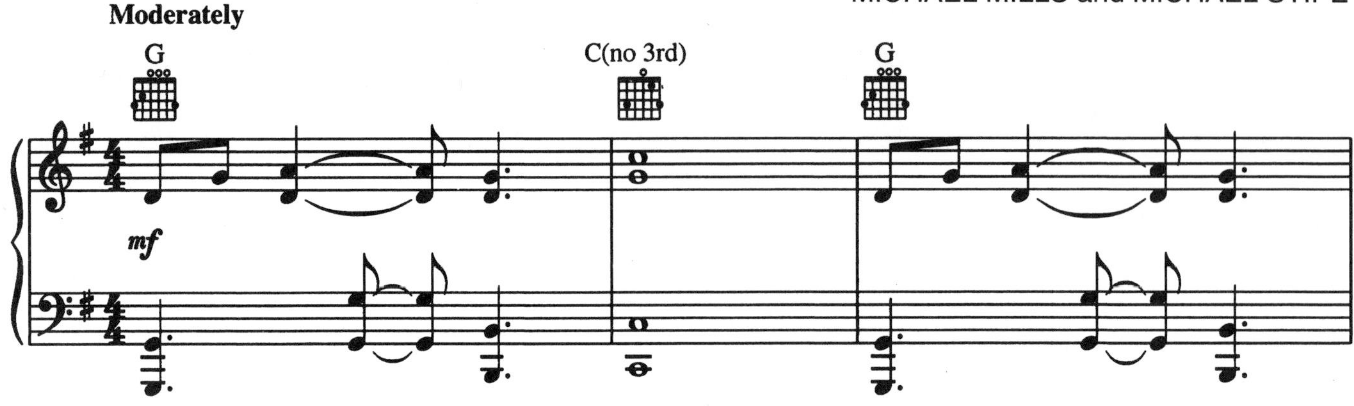
Moderately
G
C(no 3rd)
G
mf

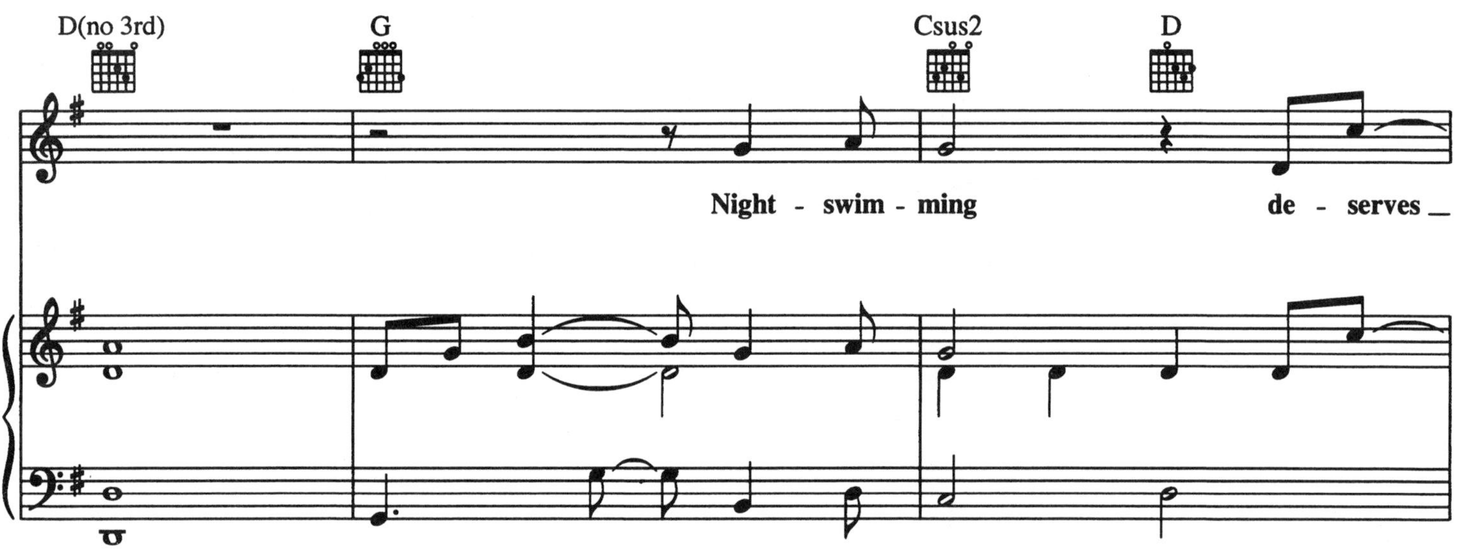
D(no 3rd)
G
Csus2
D
Night - swim - ming de - serves

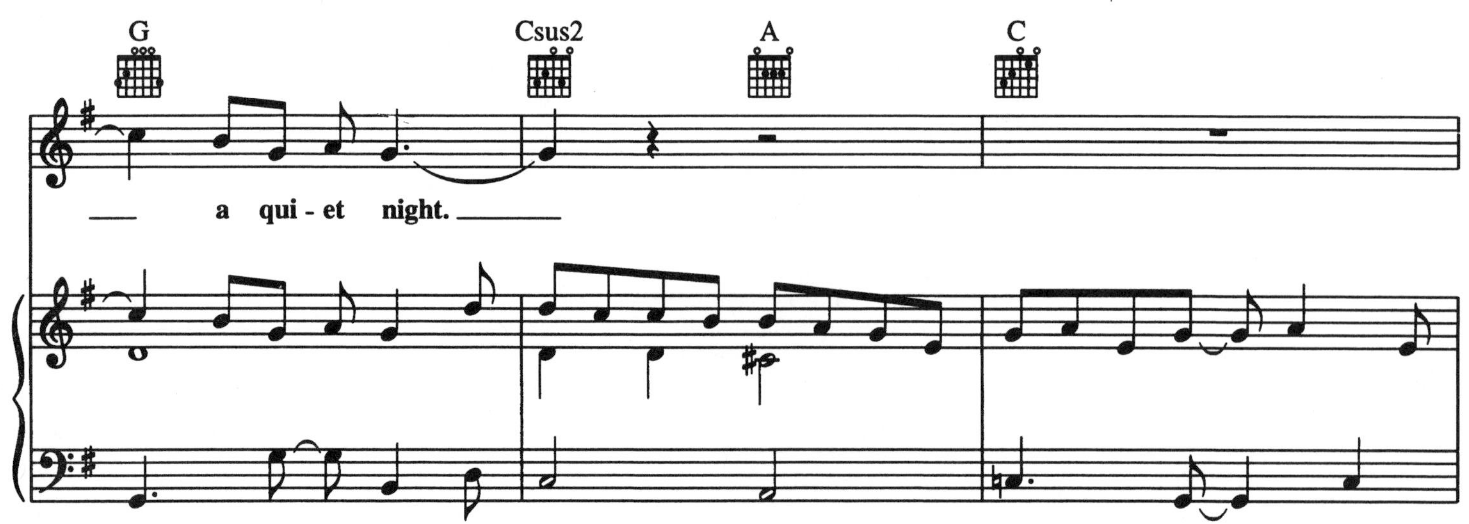
G
Csus2
A
C
a qui - et night.

Dsus
D
G
The pho - to - graph on the dash -
Csus2
D
G
- board, tak - en years a - go,
Csus2
A
C
Dsus
D
turned a - round back - wards so the wind - shield shows.
G
Csus2
D
G
Ev - er - y street - light re - veals the pic - ture in re - verse.
You, I thought I knew you. You I can - not judge.

Csus2 A C

Still, it's so much clear - er.
You, I thought you knew me,

Dsus D G Csus2 D

I for - got my shirt at the wa - ter's edge.
this one laugh-ing qui - et - ly un - der-neath my breath.

G Csus2 A C

The moon is low to - night.
Night - swim - ming.

Dsus D G C

G
D(no 3rd)
To Coda
G
Night - swim -
Night - swim -
Csus2
D
G
Csus2
A
ming de - serves a qui - et night. I'm
ming, re - mem - ber - ing that night. Sep -
C
Dsus
D
not sure all these peo - ple un - der - stand.
tem - ber's com - ing soon. I'm
G
Csus2
D
It's not like years a - go,
pin - ing for the moon. And

G
Csus2
A
the fear of get - ting caught,
what if there were two side by
C
Dsus
D
G
of reck - less - ness and wa - ter. They can -
side in or - bit a - round the fair - est sun? That
Csus2
D
G
Csus2
A
- not see me na - ked. These things, they go a - way,
bright, tight for - ev - er drum could not de - scribe night - swim -
1
C
Dsus
D
re - placed by eve - ry - day.

2
C
D
D.S. al Coda
ming.
CODA
G
C
Dsus
G
C
A
C
Dsus
D
The
G
Csus2
D
G
1. pho - to - graph _ re - flects, _ eve - ry street - light a ___ re - mind -
2. Instrumental solo

Csus2
A
C
Dsus
D
- er. Night - swim - ming de - serves a qui - et night, _
G
Csus2
D
G
Csus2
A
C
de - serves a qui - et night. _
1
Dsus
D
2
Dsus
D
G
rit.

ROCKY MOUNTAIN HIGH

Words and Music by
JOHN DENVER and MIKE TAYLOR

Moderately ♩ = 84
*Guitar Capo 2
D
Em7
G
A
Piano
E
F♯m7
A
B
mf
C
D
1. He was born
Verse:
in the sum - mer of his twen-ty - sev-enth year,
com-in'
2.–5. See additional lyrics
(Cue notes 1st time only)

*Tune 6th string down to D.

D
Em7
E
F♯m7
home to a place he'd nev - er been be - fore.
G
A
D
A
B
E
He left yes - ter - day be - hind him; you might
Em7
C
A
D
F♯m7
D
B
E
say he was born a - gain. You might say he found a key
Em7
F♯m7
1.3.
2.4.5.
G
A
G
A
A
B
A
B
for ev - 'ry door.
2. When he
4. Now he
But the

Chorus:
G A D E
Col - o - ra - do Rock - y Moun - tain high,
G A B
I've seen it rain - in' fire in the sky.
D E G A
The shad - ow from the star - light is soft - er than a lul - la - by.
Talk to God and lis - ten to the cas - u - al re - ply.
I know he'd be a poor - er man if he nev - er saw an ea - gle fly.
A B D E Em7 Dmaj7 F♯m7 Emaj7 G A

To Coda
Rock - y Moun - tain high.
D
E
Em7
F♯m7
(Bkgrd.) High,
Col - o - ra - do.
G
A
A
B
D
E
Rock - y Moun - tain high.
High,
Col - o - ra -
Em7
F♯m7
do.
1.
D.S.
2.
D.S. al Coda
G
A
A
B
G
A
A
B
3. He climbed
5. Now his life

Coda
D
E
Chorus:
G
5
A
A
7
B
D
E
Col - o - ra - do Rock - y Moun - tain high;
G
5
A
A
7
B
I've seen it rain - in' fire in the sky.
D
E
G
5
A
Friends a - round the camp-

A
D
Em7
D
G
B
E
F♯m7
E
A
fire, and ev - 'ry - bod - y's high.
Rock - y Moun - tain high.
D
Em7
G
A
E
F♯m7
A
B
(Bkgrd.) High, Col - o - ra - do.
Rock - y Moun - tain high.
Repeat ad lib. and fade
D
Em7
G
A
E
F♯m7
A
B
High, Col - o - ra - do.
Rock - y Moun - tain high.

Verse 2:
When he first came to the mountains, his life was far away,
On the road and hangin' by a song.
But the string's already broken and he doesn't really care.
It keeps changin' fast and it don't last for long.
(*To Chorus:*)

Verse 3:
He climbed cathedral mountains; he saw silver clouds below.
He saw everything as far as you can see.
And they say that he got crazy once and he tried to touch the sun,
And he lost a friend, but kept the memory.

Verse 4:
Now he walks in quiet solitude, the rivers and the streams,
Seeking grace in every step he takes.
His sight has turned inside himself to try and understand
The serenity of a clear blue mountain lake.
(*To Chorus:*)

Verse 5:
Now his life is full of wonder but his heart still knows some fear
Of a simple thing he cannot comprehend.
Why they try to tear the mountains down to bring in a couple more,
More people, more scars upon the land.
(*To Chorus:*)

NOBODY HOME

Words and Music by
ROGER WATERS

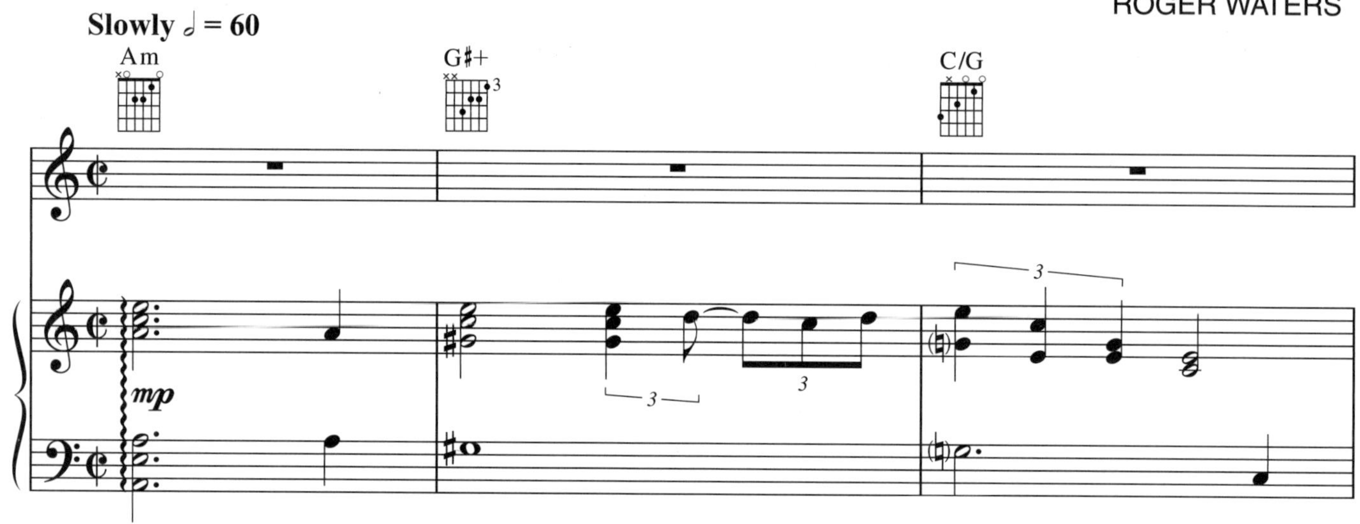
Slowly 𝅗𝅥 = 60
Am
G♯+
C/G
mp
3

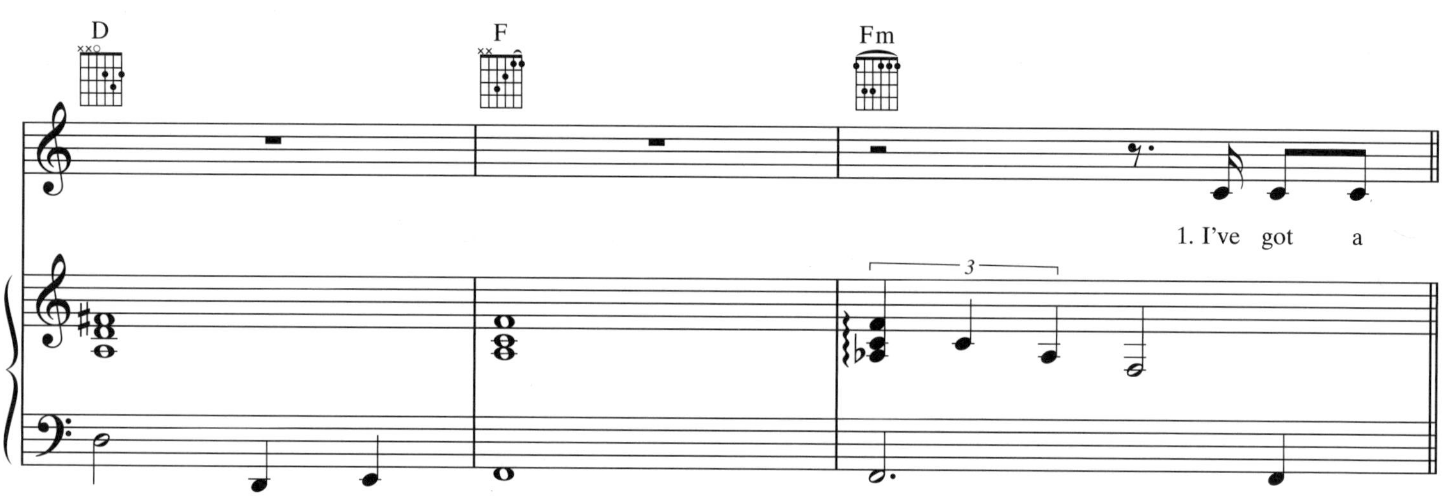
D
F
Fm
3
1. I've got a

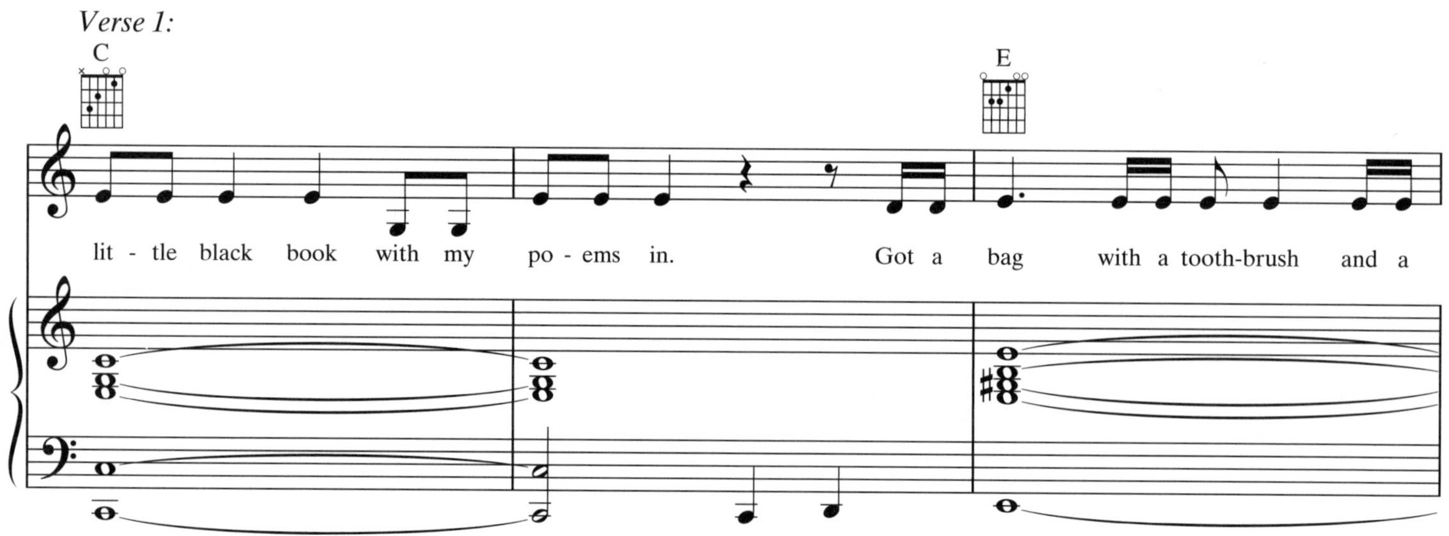
Verse 1:
C
E
lit - tle black book with my po - ems in. Got a bag with a tooth-brush and a

E7
F
comb in. When I'm a good dog, they some-times throw me a
C
F/C
C
bone in. I've got e - las - tic bands keep - ing my shoes
E
E7
on. Got those swol - len hand blues. I got
F
C
thir - teen chan-nels of sh*t on the T V to choose from. I've got e -

C7
lec - tric light,
and I've got sec - ond sight. I've got a -
cresc.
F
Fm/C
C
G/B
Am
D7/F♯
maz - ing pow - ers of ob - ser - va - tion.
G
E7/G♯
Am
G+
And that is how I know, when I try to get through
8va
C/G
D/F♯
on the tel - e - phone to you,
dim.

Fm6
C
F
C
there'll be no - bod - y home.
cresc.
Verse 2:
F
C
2. I've got the ob - lig - a - to - ry Hen - drix perm, and the in -
mf
E
F
3
ev - i - ta - ble pin - hole burns all down the front of my
C
F
C
fav - o - rite sat - in shirt. I've got nic - o - tine stains on my

E
fin - gers. I've got a sil - ver spoon on a chain. Got a
F
C
grand pi - an - o to prop up my mor - tal re - mains. I've got
C7
wild, star - ing eyes, and I've got a strong urge to fly,
F
Fm
C
G/B
Am
D7/F♯
but I've got no-where to fly to.

G
E7/G♯
Am
Ooh,
babe,
C/G
D/F♯
Fm6
when I pick up the phone,
there's still no - bod - y
dim.
C
F
C
F
home.
I've got a
C
E
E7
pair of Go - hills boots,
but I've got
fad - ing roots.
rit.

THE ONLY EXCEPTION

Words and Music by
HAYLEY WILLIAMS and JOSH FARRO

Slowly ♩. = 48
B
mf

F♯m6
Emaj7

B

F♯m6
Emaj7

Verse 1 (sing 1st time only):
B
F♯m6
1. When I was youn - ger, I saw my dad - dy cry and curse at the wind.
Verse 2 (sing 2nd time only):
(2.) may - be I know some - where deep in my soul that love nev - er lasts.
Emaj7
B
He broke his own heart, and I watched as he tried to re -
And we've got to find oth - er ways to make it a - lone,
F♯m6
Emaj7
B
as - sem - ble it. And my ma - ma swore that she
or keep a straight face. And I've al - ways lived like

F♯m6
would nev - er let her - self for - get.
this, keep - ing a com - f'ta - ble
Emaj7
B
And that was the day that I
dis - tance. And up un - til now I had sworn
F♯m6
prom - ised I'd nev - er sing of love if it does not ex -
to my - self that I'm con - tent with lone - li - ness,

1.
To Next Strain
2.
Emaj7
Emaj7
ist. But, dar - lin', because none of it was ev - er worth the risk. Well,
Chorus:
B
(sing harmony 2nd time)
you are the on - ly ex - cep - tion. Well,
F♯m6
Emaj7
you are the on - ly ex - cep - tion. Well,
B
you are the on - ly ex - cep - tion. Well,

1.
F♯m6
Emaj7
you are the on - ly ex - cep - tion.
B
2.
Emaj7
2. Well, on - ly ex - cep - tion.
C♯m9
B
F♯
C♯m9
B
F♯
I've got a

Bridge:
C#m9
tight grip on re - al - i - ty, but I can't let
B
F#
go of what's in front of me here. I know you're
C#m9
leav - ing in the morn - ing when you wake up. Leave me
B
F#
with some kind of proof it's not a dream. Oh.

Emaj9
Chorus:
B
(sing harmony 2nd time)
You are the on - ly ex - cep - tion.
F♯m6
Emaj7
You are the on - ly ex - cep - tion.
B
You are the on - ly ex - cep - tion. Well,

1.
F♯m6
Emaj7
you are the on - ly ex - cep - tion.
2.
F♯m6
Emaj7
A
you are the on - ly ex - cep - tion. And I'm on my
Emaj7
B
way to be - liev - ing.
Oh, and
A
Emaj7
B
I'm on my way to be - liev - ing.
mp

PEACEFUL EASY FEELING

Words and Music by
JACK TEMPCHIN

Moderately
E
Esus4
E
A
mf
I like the way your spar-klin' ear-
E
A
E
A
B
rings lay a-gainst your skin so brown,
A
E
A
E
and I wan-na sleep with you in the des-ert to-night

A
E
A
B
Bsus4
2 fr.
B
with a bil - lion stars all_ a-round.
'Cause I got a
A
E
A
peace - ful
eas - y feel - in',
and I know you won't_
F#m7
B
E
F#m7
A
let me_ down,
'cause I'm al - read-y stand - in'
Bsus4
2 fr.
E
Esus4
E
Esus4
on the ground.

E
A
E
A
And I found out a long time a-go
E
A
B
Bsus4
2 fr.
B
Bsus4
2 fr.
what a wom-an can do to your soul,
E
A
E
A
ah, but she can't take you an - y-way,
E
A
B
you don't al-read-y know how to go.
And I got a

A
E
peace - ful easy - y feel - in',
A
Bsus4
2 fr.
B
and I know you won't let me down, 'cause I'm
E
F#m7
A
To Coda
Bsus4
2 fr.
al - read-y stand - in' on the ground.
E
Esus4
E
Esus4

E
A
E
A
I get this feel - in' I may know you
E
A
B
as a lov - er and a friend,
E
A
E
A
but this voice keeps whis - per - ing in my oth - er ear, tells me
D.S. 𝄋 al Coda ⊕
E
A
B
Bsus4
2 fr.
B
I may nev - er see you a - gain. 'Cause I get a

Coda
Bsus4
2 fr.
E
F#m7
A
Bsus4
2 fr.
E
I'm __ al - read-y stand-in', yes, I'm __ al -
F#m7
A
Bsus4
2 fr.
E
F#m7
read-y stand-in' on the ground. ______
A
B
E
F#m7
A
Whoa. ______
B
E
F#m7
A
B
E
rit.

Gtr. tuned down 1/2 step:
⑥ = E♭ ③ = G♭
⑤ = A♭ ② = B♭
④ = D♭ ① = E♭

PHOTOGRAPH

Lyrics by
CHAD KROEGER

Music by
NICKELBACK

Moderately slow ♩ = 76
Verse:
Guitar → E5
Piano → E♭5
B(4)
B♭(4)
1. Look at this pho - to - graph, ev - 'ry time I do, it makes me laugh.
mf
D6/9
D♭6/9
A(9)
A♭(9)
How did our eyes get so red? And what the hell is on Jo - ey's head?
E5
E♭5
B(4)
B♭(4)
And this is where I grew up, I think the pres - ent own - er fixed it up.
2. Re - mem - ber the old ar - cade? Blew ev - 'ry dol - lar that we ev - er made.

D6/9 — A(9)

D♭6/9 — A♭(9)

I never knew we ever went without, the second floor is hard for sneaking out.
The cops hated us hangin' out, they said somebody went and burned it down.

E5 — B(4)

E♭5 — B♭(4)

And this is where I went to school, most of the time, had better things to do.
We used to listen to the radio, and sing along with ev'ry song we'd know.

D6/9 — A(9)

D♭6/9 — A♭(9)

Criminal record says I broke in twice, I must have done it half a dozen times.
We said someday we'd find out how it feels to sing to more than just the steering wheel.

E5 — B(4)

E♭5 — B♭(4)

I wonder if it's too late, should I go back and try to graduate?
Kim's the first girl I kissed, I was so nervous that I nearly missed.

D6/9
A(9)
D♭6/9
A♭(9)
Life's bet - ter now than it was back then, if I was them, I would-n't let me in.
She's had a cou - ple of kids since then, I have-n't seen her since God knows when.
G6
A(9)
G♭6
A♭(9)
Oh, whoa, whoa, oh, God, I, I. Ev - 'ry
Chorus:
E5
B(4)
E♭5
B♭(4)
mem-o - ry of look-ing out the back door, I had the pho - to al - bum spread out on the bed - room floor. It's
D6/9
A(9)
D♭6/9
A♭(9)
hard to say it, time to say it, good - bye, good - bye. Ev - 'ry

E5
Eb5
B(4)
Bb(4)
mem-o-ry of walk-ing out the front door, I found a pho-to of the friend that I was look-ing for. It's
D6/9
Db6/9
To Coda
1.
A(9)
Ab(9)
hard to say it, time to say it, good-bye, good-bye.
2.
A(9)
Ab(9)
Cmaj7
Cbmaj7
good-bye, good-bye.
D6/9
Db6/9
Bridge:
E5
Eb5
I miss that town,

B(4)
G6
B♭(4)
G♭6
I miss their fac - es. You can't e - rase,
A(9)
E5
A♭(9)
E♭5
you can't re - place it. I miss it now,
B(4)
G6
B♭(4)
G♭6
I can't be - lieve it. So hard to stay,
A(9)
E5
A♭(9)
E♭5
too hard to leave it. If I could re - live those days,

B(4)
D6/9
D.S. 𝄋 al Coda
B♭(4)
D♭6/9
I know the one thing that would nev - er change.
Ev - 'ry
Coda
A(9)
E5
A♭(9)
E♭5
good - bye, good - bye.
Look at this pho - to - graph.
B(4)
D6/9
A(9)
B♭(4)
D♭6/9
A♭(9)
Ev-'ry time I do, it makes me laugh.
Ev-'ry time I do, it makes me...

RUBY TUESDAY

Words and Music by
MICK JAGGER and KEITH RICHARDS

Slowly ♩= 92
Verse:
B♭m
B♭m7/A♭
G♭
A♭
1. She would nev - er say where she came from.
(2.) ques - tion why she needs to be so free.
3. "There's no time to lose," I heard her say.
mf
D♭sus
D♭
D♭sus
D♭
B♭m
B♭m7/A♭
Yes - ter - day don't
She'll tell you it's the on
Catch your dreams be-fore
G♭
D♭
A♭7
mat-ter if it's gone.
- ly way to be.
they slip a - way.

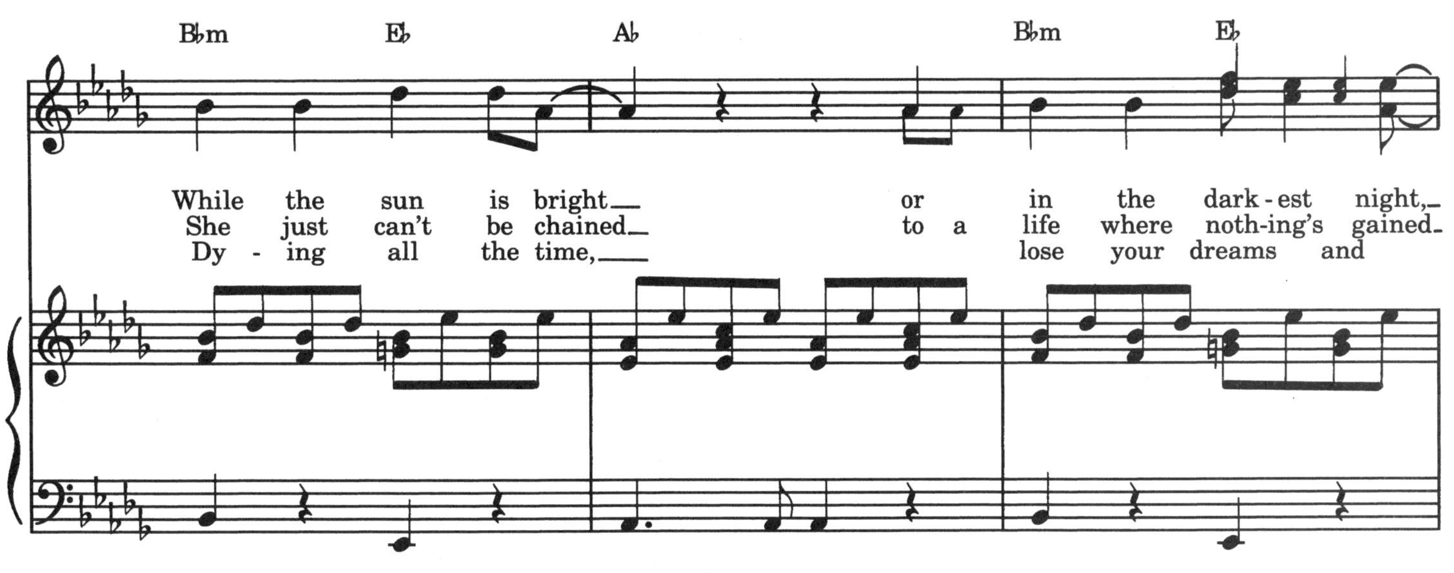
B♭m
E♭
A♭
B♭m
E♭
While the sun is bright or in the dark-est night,
She just can't be chained to a life where noth-ing's gained.
Dy - ing all the time, lose your dreams and

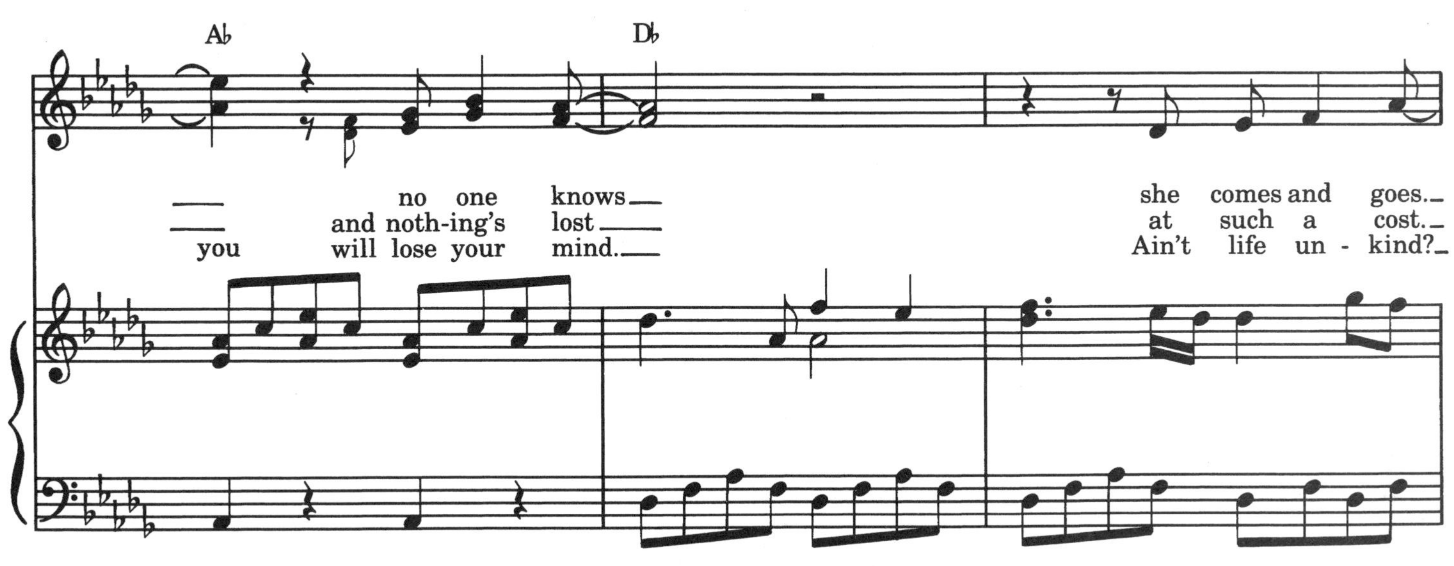
A♭
D♭
no one knows she comes and goes.
and noth-ing's lost at such a cost.
you will lose your mind. Ain't life un - kind?

Chorus:
D♭
A♭
Good - bye,
cresc.
f

D♭
A♭
D♭
Ru - by Tues - day.
Who could_hang a name_ on you?_
D♭
A♭7
C♭
G♭
A♭
D♭
When you_change with ev - 'ry new_ day.
Still, I'm gon-na miss you.
1. 2.
A♭
(2.) Don't
3.
D.S. 𝄋
4.
A♭
Recorder
B♭m
B♭m7/A♭
G♭maj7
A♭
D♭
rall.

SATURDAY IN THE PARK

Words and Music by
ROBERT LAMM

Moderately ♩ = 120
Am7 Am7(4) D9 D7 Fmaj7/G G9sus C Am7
mf
(L.H. continue in octaves)
Am7(4) D9 D7 Fmaj7/G G9sus C Am7
Am7(4) D9 D7 Fmaj7/G G9sus C Am7
(Horns)

© 1970 (Renewed) SPIRIT SERVICES HOLDINGS, S.à.r.l., BIG ELK MUSIC and LAMMINATIONS MUSIC
All Rights for SPIRIT SERVICES HOLDINGS, S.à.r.l. and BIG ELK MUSIC
Controlled and Administered by SPIRIT TWO MUSIC, INC. (ASCAP)
All Rights Reserved Used by Permission

Verse 1:
Am7(4)
D9
D7
Fmaj7/G
G9sus
C
Am7
1. Sat - ur - day in the park, I think it was the Fourth of Ju - ly.
Sat - ur - day in the park, I think it was the Fourth of Ju - ly.
Bm7
Em7
Dmaj7
Peo - ple danc - ing, peo - ple laugh - ing, a man sell - ing ice cream,
(No octaves)
C
D
G
G7sus
C/G
sing - ing I - tal - ian songs. (Ei - cay va - re, ei - se nar - de.) Can

G Am7

___ you dig___ it? Yes, I___ can.___ And I've been wait - ing such a long time______ for

D9 G

Sat - ur - day.______________

(Horns)

C

Verse 2:

Am7 Am7(4) D9 D7 Fmaj7/G

2. An - oth - er day___ in the park,___ I

8vb

(L.H. continue in octaves)

G9sus C Am7 Am7(4) D9 D7 Fmaj7/G

think it was the Fourth of Ju - ly.______ An - oth - er day___ in the park,_ I

G9sus
C
Bm7
Em7
think it was the Fourth of Ju - ly.
Peo - ple talk - ing, real - ly smil - ing, a
(No octaves)
Dmaj7
C
D
man play - ing gui - tar
and sing - ing for us all.
G
G7sus
C/G
G
Will you help him change the world? Can you dig it? Yes, I can. And I've been
Am7
D9
wait - ing such a long time
for to - day.

Swing
Bridge:
C11 C C11 C C11 C C11 C
Slow mo - tion rid - ers fly the col - ors of the day. A
Eb11 Eb Eb11 Eb Eb11 Eb Eb11 Eb
bronze man still can tell sto - ries his own way.
Fmaj7/G G Fmaj7/G G Fmaj7/G G Fmaj7/G G Fmaj7/G
Lis-ten, chil - dren, all is not lost, all is not lost, oh, no, no.
Tempo I
Am7 Am7(4) D9 D7 Fmaj7/G G9sus C Dm/C Cm7 Dm/C
(L.H. continue in octaves)

Am7
Am7(4)
D9
D7
Fmaj7/G
G9sus
C
(Horns)
Verse 3:
3. Fun - ny days in the park; ev-'ry day's the Fourth of Ju - ly.
Fun - ny days in the park; ev-'ry day's the Fourth of Ju - ly.
Bm7
Em7
Dmaj7
Peo-ple reach - ing, peo-ple touch - ing, a real cel - e - bra - tion
(No octaves)

C
D
G
G7sus
C/G
wait-ing for__ us all.____
Wait-ing for__ us all.____
(Bkgrd.)
If you want_ it, real - ly want_ it, can_
G
Am7
__ you dig__ it? Yes, I___ can._ And I've been wait-ing such a long time______
D9
G
for the day,______ yeah,______ yeah,_ ooh,______ mm,______
C
______ mm.______

Tune Guitar to "Open E":
⑥ = E ③ = G♯
⑤ = B ② = B
④ = E ① = E

SHE TALKS TO ANGELS

Words and Music by
CHRIS ROBINSON and RICH ROBINSON

Slow ballad ♩ = 80

N.C.
E
N.C.
mf
E
A6/9
E
A6/9
E
B/E
7
E
A6/9
E
A6/9
E
A6/9
E
A6/9
E
A6/9
E
A6/9
E
1. She nev - er men - tions the word ad -

Verse 1:

A6/9 E A6/9 E

dic - tion___ in cer - tain com -

A6/9 E A6/9 E

pa - ny.___ Yes, she'll tell you she's an

A6/9 E A6/9 E

or - phan___ af - ter you meet her fam -

A6/9 E A6/9 E

i - ly.___

B
E/B
B
A
E
A6/9
E
A6/9
E
B
E/B
B
A
E
A6/9
E
A6/9
E
E
A6/9
E
A6/9
E
2. She paints her eyes as black as

Verses 2, 3, & 4:
A6/9
E
(2.4.) night, now,
3. See additional lyrics
pulls those shades down tight.
Yeah, she gives a smile when the
pain comes.
The pain gon - na make ev - 'ry-thing al - right.
Says she talks to

Chorus:
B
E/B
B
A
an - gels.
They call her out by
E
A6/9
E
A6/9
E
her name.
Oh, yeah, she talks to
B
E/B
B
A
To Coda
an - gels.
Says they call her out by
1.
E
A6/9
E
A6/9
E
B/E
her name.

E
A6/9
E
A6/9
E
3. She keeps a lock of hair in her
2.
E
A6/9
E
A6/9
E
her name.
Bridge:
A
B/A
A
E
A/E
E
A
B/A
A
E
She don't know no lov - er,
none that I ev - er seen.
A/E
E
A
B/A
A
E
A/E
E
Yeah, to her that ain't noth - in',
but to me

A2
it
means,
means
ev
-
'ry
-
thing.
E
A6/9
E
A6/9
E
B/E
E
A6/9
E
A6/9
E
A6/9
E
A6/9
E

D.S. 𝄋 al Coda
A6/9 E A6/9 E
4. She paints her eyes as black as
Coda
E A6/9 E A6/9 E
her name.
Oh,
B E/B B A
an - gels,
they call her out by
E A6/9 E A6/9 E
her name.
Oh, oh, she talks to

B
E/B
B
A
an - gels.
They call her out,
yeah, yeah,
call her out.
Don't you know that they
call her out
by
her
name?
E
E

Verse 3:
She keeps a lock of hair in her pocket.
She wears a cross around her neck.
The hair is from a little boy,
And the cross from someone she has not met.
Well, not yet.
(To Chorus:)

Verse 4:
Repeat 2nd Verse

SONG FROM M*A*S*H
(Suicide Is Painless)

Words and Music by
MIKE ALTMAN and JOHNNY MANDEL

Folk - Gospel pop feel ♩ = 108
Am
Am9
G/A
mf
1. Through
Verse:
Dm7
G7sus
G7
Cmaj7
ear - ly morn - ing fog I see vi - sions of the
try to find a way to make all our lit - tle
3.4.5.6. See additional lyrics
things to be. The pains that are with - held for me I
joys re - late with - out that ev - er pres - ent hate. But

C
Am9
G/A
A7
re - al - ize and I can see that
now I know that it's too late and
Chorus:
Dm7
G7
C(9)
Am9
su - i - cide is pain - less. It brings on man - y chang - es, and
Fmaj7
C/E
Dm7
Dm7/G
1.2.3.4.5.
Am
Am9
I can take or leave it if I please.
2. I
6.
G/A
And
rall.
poco a poco molto rall.

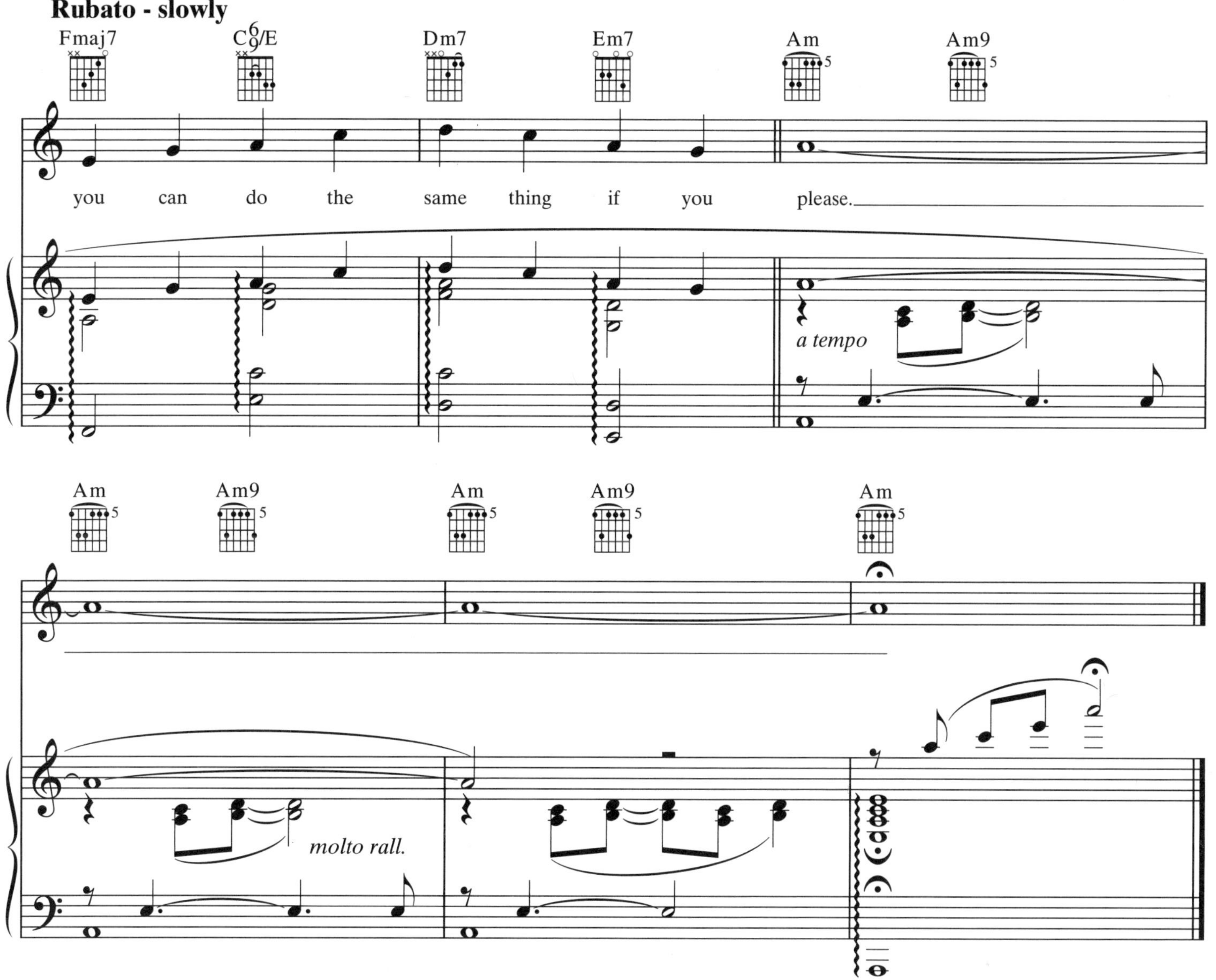
Rubato - slowly
Fmaj7
C6/9/E
Dm7
Em7
Am
Am9
you can do the same thing if you please.
a tempo
Am
Am9
Am
Am9
Am
molto rall.

Verse 3:
The game of life is hard to play.
I'm going to lose it anyway.
The losing card I'll someday lay,
So this is all I have to say.
That:
(To Chorus:)

Verse 4:
The only way to win is cheat
And lay it down before I'm beat,
And to another give a seat
For that's the only painless feat.
'Cause:
(To Chorus:)

Verse 5:
The sword of time will pierce our skins.
It doesn't hurt when it begins,
But as it works its way on in,
The pain grows stronger, watch it grin.
For:
(To Chorus:)

Verse 6:
A brave man once requested me
To answer questions that are key.
Is it to be or not to be?
And I replied; "Oh, why ask me?"
'Cause:
(To Chorus:)

SHOWER THE PEOPLE

Words and Music by
JAMES TAYLOR

Moderately
Guitar → D
(capo 3rd fret)
Piano → F
mf
You can play the game and you can act out the part though you know it was-n't writ-ten for you. But tell me how can you stand there with your bro-ken heart a-shamed of play-ing the fool.
You can run but you can-not hide; this is wide-ly known. And what you plan to do with your fool-ish pride when you're all by your-self a-lone.
A C
Bm Dm
D/A F/C
G B♭
D F
A C
A♯o7 C♯o7
Bm Dm
D/A F/C

G D A
B♭ F C
One thing can lead to an - oth - er; it does-n't
Once you tell some-bod-y the way that you feel you can
Bm D/A G D
Dm F/C B♭ F
take an - y sac - ri - fice. Oh, fa - ther and moth - er, sis -
feel it be-gin-ning to ease. I think it's true what they say a-bout the
A A#o7 Bm D/A G D/F#
C C#o7 Dm F/C B♭ F/A
ter and broth - er, if it feels nice don't think twice. Just
squeak - y wheel, al-ways get - ting the grease. Bet - ter to
Em7 A Em7
Gm7 C Gm7
show-er the peo - ple you love with love; show them the way that you feel.

A
Em7
A
A#º7
C
Gm7
C
C#º7
Things are gon - na { work out / be just } fine, if you on - ly will.
Bm
F#º7
Em7
A
Dm
Aº7
Gm7
C
Show-er the peo-ple you love with love;
Em7
A
Em7
Gm7
C
Gm7
show them the way you feel.
Things are gon - na be much bet-
A
A#º7
1.
Bm
C
G
C
C#º7
Dm
E♭
B♭
ter if you on - ly will.

2.
Bm
Dm
No chord
Repeat and fade (with vocal ad lib)
N. C.
Show - er the peo - ple you love with love;
Repeat and fade
show them the way that you feel.

Vocal Ad Lib

They say in every life,
They say the rain must fall.
Just like a pouring rain,
Make it rain.
Love is sunshine.

THE SOUND OF SILENCE

Words and Music by
PAUL SIMON

Moderately ♩ = 104

Guitar Capo 7 ⟶ * *A2*

Piano ⟶ E2

Verse 1:

G
D

1. Hel-lo, dark-ness, my old friend,

mp legato

Am
Em

C
G

I've come with talk__ to you a - gain. Be-cause a vi - sion soft - ly__

F
C
C
G
F
C
C
G
__ creep-ing__
left its seeds while I was____ sleep - ing.__

*Original recording in E♭m, capo at the 6th fret.

F
C
Am
C
G
Em
And the vi - sion that was plant-ed in my brain still re - mains
C
G
A2
G
D
E2
with-in the sound of si - lence.
2. In rest - less dreams I walked a -
Verse 2:
G
Am
D
Em
lone, nar - row streets of cob-ble - stone. 'Neath the ha - lo of a
F
C
F
C
C
G
C
G
street - lamp I turned my col - lar to the cold and damp,

F
C
C
G
when my eyes were stabbed by the flash of a ne-on light that split the
Am
C
G
Am
Em
G
D
Em
night and touched the sound of si-lence.
Verse 3:
G
D
Am
Em
3. And in the na-ked light I saw ten thou-sand peo-ple, may-be more.
C
F
C
F
C
G
C
G
C
G
Peo-ple talk-ing with-out speak-ing, peo-ple hear-ing with-out lis-t'ning.

F C
C G
Peo-ple writ-ing songs that voic-es nev-er share__ and no one
Am C G Am
Em G D Em
dared dis-turb the sound of si-lence.
Verse 4:
G Am
D Em
4. "Fools," said I, "you do not know, si-lence like a can-cer grows.
F C F C
C G C G
Hear my words that I might__ teach you,__ take my arms that I might__ reach you."__

F
C
C
G
But my words like si - lent rain - drops fell
Am
C
G
Em
G
D
and ech - oed in the wells of
Verse 5:
Am
G
Em
D
si - lence.
5. And the peo - ple bowed and prayed
Am
Em
to the ne - on god they made.
And the sign flashed out its

F C F C
C G C G
warn - ing in the words that it was form - ing.
F
C
And the sign said, "The words of the proph - ets are writ - ten on the sub - way walls
C Am C
G Em G
and ten - e - ment halls" and whis - pered in the
G A2 Am
D E2 Em
sounds of si - lence.
rit.

STAIRWAY TO HEAVEN

Words and Music by
JIMMY PAGE and ROBERT PLANT

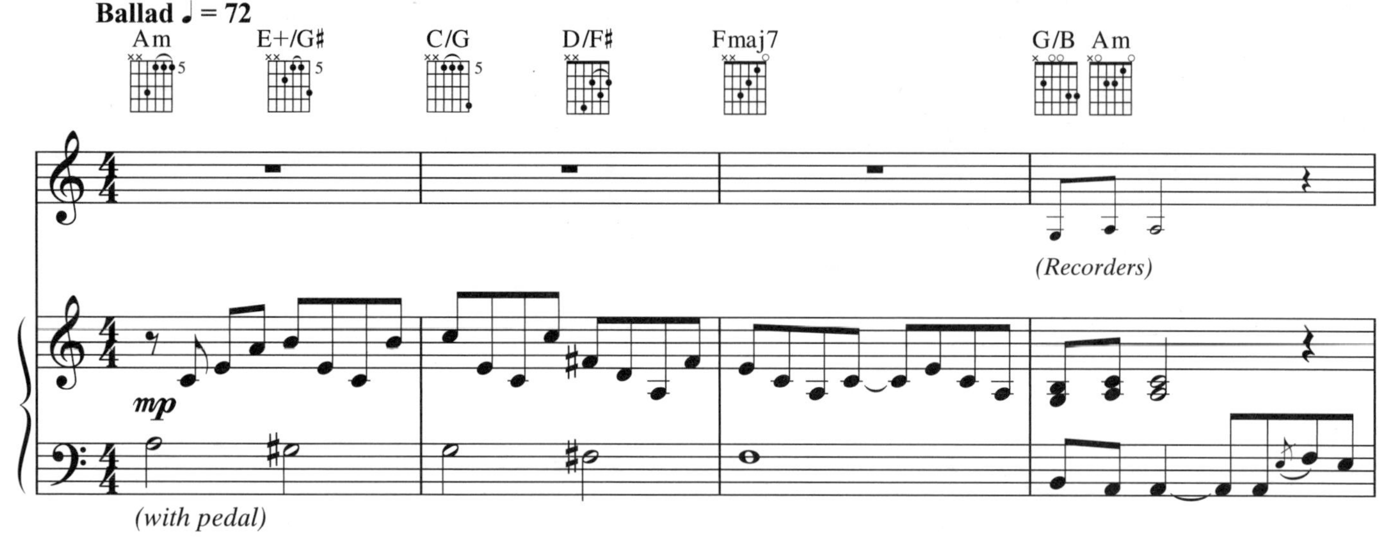
Ballad ♩ = 72
Am
E+/G♯
C/G
D/F♯
Fmaj7
G/B
Am
(Recorders)
mp
(with pedal)

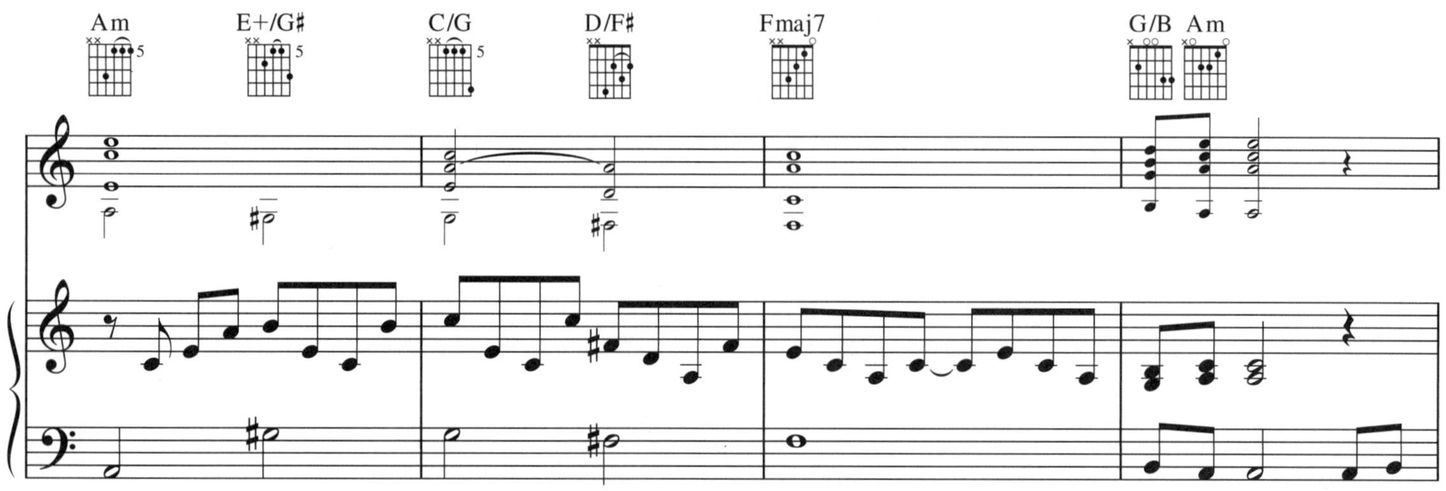
Am
E+/G♯
C/G
D/F♯
Fmaj7
G/B
Am

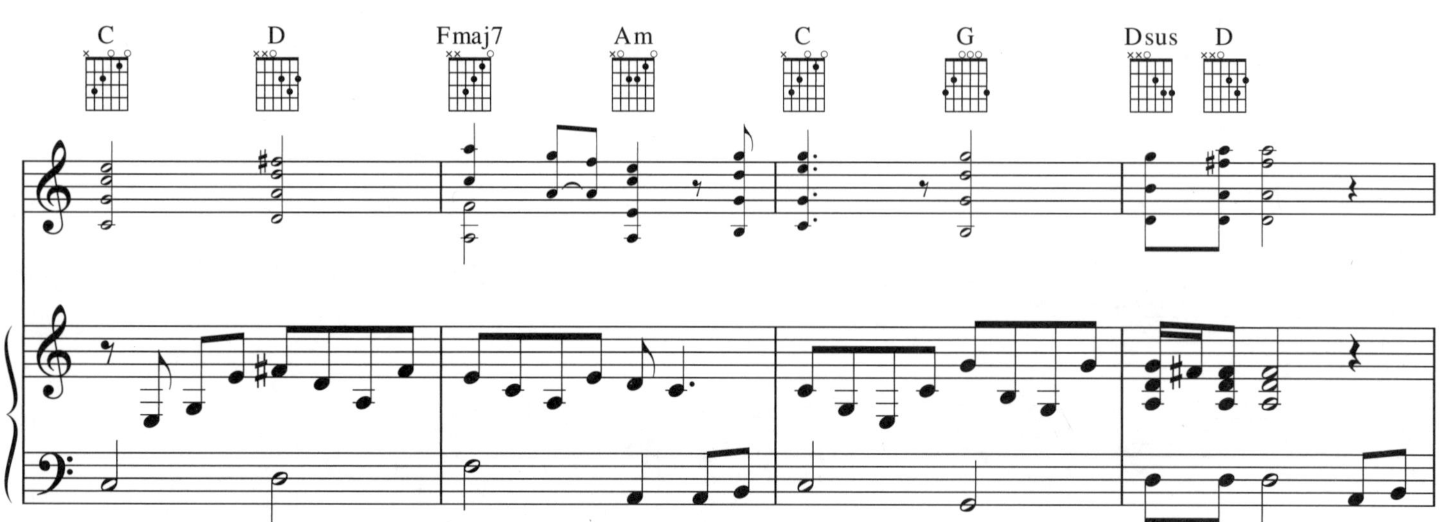
C
D
Fmaj7
Am
C
G
Dsus
D

C
D
Fmaj7
Am
C
D
Fmaj7
1. There's a
Verse 1:
Am
E+/G♯
C/G
D/F♯
Fmaj7
la - dy who's sure all that glit - ters is gold,_ and she's buy - ing_ a stair-way to
G/B
Am
Am
E+/G♯
C/G
D/F♯
heav - en. When she gets there, she knows_ if the stores are all closed,_ with a
Fmaj7
G/B
Am
C
D
word she_ can get what she came_ for. Ooo,_____

Fmaj7 Am C G Dsus D
ooo, ooo, and she's buy - ing a stair - way to heav - en. There's a
C D Fmaj7 Am C D
sign on the wall, but she wants to be sure, 'cause you know some - times words have two
Fmaj7 Am E+/G♯ C/G D/F♯
mean - ings. In a tree by the brook, there's a song - bird who sings, some - times
Fmaj7 G/B Am Am E+/G♯
all of our thoughts are mis - giv - en.

C/G
D/F♯
Fmaj7
G/B
Am
G/B
Slightly faster
Am7
Dsus
D
Am7
Em/D
Ooo, it makes me won - der.
D
C/D
D
Am7
Dsus
D
Ooo, makes me won - der.
Am7
Em/D
D
C/D
D
2. There's a

Verses 2 & 3:
C G/B Am C G/B Fmaj7
feel - ing I get when I look to the west, and my spir - it is cry - ing for leav -
whis - pered that soon if we all call the tune, then the pip - er will lead us to rea -
Am C G/B Am
ing. In my thoughts I have seen rings of smoke through the trees, and the
son. And a new day will dawn, for those who stand long, and the
C G/B Fmaj7 Am C G/B
voic - es of those who stand look - ing.
for - ests will ech - o with laugh - ter.
Am7 Dsus D Am7 Em/D
Ooh, it makes me won - der.

D
C/D
D
Am7
Dsus
D
Ooo, it real-ly makes me won - der.
Am7
Em/D
1.
D
C/D
D
2.
D
C/D
D
3. And it's
accel.
Faster (♩ = 88)
Verses 4 & 5:
C
G/B
Am
C
G/B
Fmaj7
4. If there's a bus - tle in your hedge-row, don't be a - larmed now, it's just a spring clean for the May
5. Your head is hum-ming and it won't go, in case you don't know, the pip-er's call - ing you to join
mf
Am
C
G/B
Am
Queen. Yes, there are two paths you can go by, but in the long run,
him. Dear la - dy, can you hear the wind blow, and did you know,

C
G/B
Fmaj7
Am
C
G/B
there's still time to change the road you're on.
your stair - way lies on the whis - p'rin' wind.
1.
Am7
Dsus
D
Am7
Em/D
And it makes me won - der,
D
C/D
D
Am7
Dsus
D
ahh.
Am7
Em/D
D
C/D
D
2. D

D2 D Dsus
D2 D Dsus
D C(9)
C(9)#11 C(9)
C(9)#11 C(9)
f
D2 D Dsus
D2 D Dsus
D C(9)
C(9)#11 C(9)
G/B
Guitar Solo:
Am C/G
F Fmaj7
Am C/G
F Fmaj7
Am C/G
F Fmaj7

Am
C/G
F
Fmaj7
Am
C/G
F
Fmaj7
Am
C/G
F
Fmaj7
Am
C/G
Fmaj7
Am
C/G

Fmaj7
Am
C/G
Fmaj7
Am
C/G
Fmaj7
Am
G
F
G
Am
G
And as we wind_ on down the road,__
our shad - ows tall - er than our soul.__
F
G
Am
G
F
G
There walks a la - dy we all know,____

Am
G
F
G
Am
G
who shines white light and wants to show_ how ev - 'ry - thing_ still turns to
F
G
Am
G
F
G
gold._____ And if you lis - ten ver - y hard,_____
Am
G
F
G
Am
G
Fmaj7
the tune will come to you_ at last._____ When all are one_ and one is all,_

Am
G
Fmaj7
to be a rock_ and not to roll._
Am
C/G
Fmaj7
Am
C/G
Fmaj7
Am
C/G
Fmaj7
Am
C/G
rit.
Fmaj7
N.C.
And she's buy - ing a stair - way_ to heav - en._
mf

THE STORY

Words and Music by
PHIL HANSEROTH

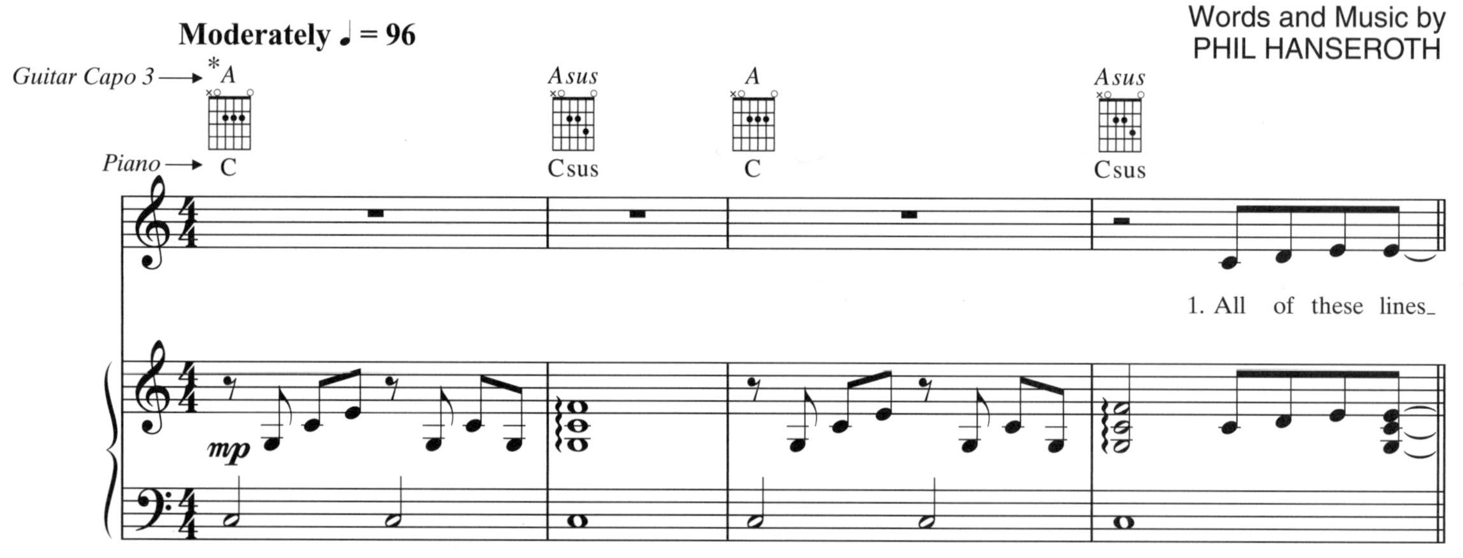
Moderately ♩ = 96
Guitar Capo 3 → *A
Asus
A
Asus
Piano → C
Csus
C
Csus
mp
1. All of these lines

Verse 1:
A
E7
C
G7
a - cross my face
tell you the sto - ry of who I am.

F#m
Am
So man-y sto - ries of where I've been
and how I got

*Original recording in B major, Guitar capo 2.

D(9)
A
F(9)
C
to where I am.
But these sto - ries don't mean
E7
F♯m
D(9)
G7
Am
F(9)
an - y - thing when you've got no one to tell them to. It's
A
E7
A
D/A
A
C
G7
C
F/C
C
true, I was made for you.
2. I climbed a - cross
Verses 2 & 3:
E7
G7
the moun - tain tops, swam all a - cross the o - cean blue.
3. (Inst. solo ad lib....
f

F♯m
Am
I crossed all the lines, and I broke all the rules, but, ba - by, I broke
D(9)
F(9)
A
C
them all for you. Oh, be-cause e - ven when I was
E7
G7
F♯m
Am
D(9)
F(9)
flat broke, you made me feel like a mil - lion bucks. You
A
C
Asus
Csus
E7
G7
1.
do. I was made for you.

2.
Verse 4:
A
C
4. You see the smile that's on my mouth? It's hid - ing the words
...end solo)
mp
E7
G7
that don't come out.
F♯m
Am
All of my friends who think that I'm blessed,
D(9)
F(9)
they don't know my head is a mess.
No,
A
C
E7
G7
F♯m
Am
they don't know who I real - ly am. And they don't know what I've
mf

D(9)
F(9)
A
C
E7
G7
been through like you do. And I was made for you.
A
C
D/A
F/C
A
C
Verse 5:
5. All of these lines a - cross my face
f
E7
G7
tell you the sto - ry of who I am. So man - y sto -
F♯m
Am
D(9)
F(9)
ries of where I've been and how I got to where I am.

A E7
C G7

___ Oh,__ but these sto-ries don't_ mean an - y - thing___ when you've

F♯m D(9) A Asus
Am F(9) C Csus

got no one__ to tell them to.______ It's true,______

E7 A Asus A Asus
G7 C Csus C Csus

I was made_ for___ you.____ Oh, yeah,_ well, it's

A Asus E7 A D/A A
C Csus G7 C F/C C

true that I was made_ for_____ you.______

mf

rit.

SUNDOWN

Words and Music by
GORDON LIGHTFOOT

Moderately, with a strong beat
*Guitar → E5
Piano → F5
mf
I can
E5
F
B7sus4
C7sus4
see her ly-in' back in her sat-in dress in a room where you do what you
pic-ture ev-'ry move that a man could make; get-tin' lost in her lov-in' is your
E5
F
A
B♭
don't con-fess.
first mis-take.
Sun-down, you bet-ter take care if I
Sun-down, you bet-ter take care if I

* Guitarists: Please note that the chord diagrams are in the key of E but the piano accompaniment is in the key of F. In order for the guitar to sound in the same key as the piano, use a capo on the 1st fret. You also may adjust the capo to play in any key that fits your own individual vocal range.

D
E5
E♭
F
find you bin creep-in' round my back stairs.
find you bin creep-in' round my back stairs.
Sun - down, you
Some - times I
A
D
E5
B♭
E♭
F
bet - ter take care if I find you bin creep-in' round my back stairs.
think it's a sin when I feel like I'm win-nin' when I'm los - in' a - gain.
E5
F
She's bin look-in' like a queen in a sail-or's dream, and she
I can see her look-in' fast in her fad - ed jeans; she's a
B7sus4
C7sus4
E5
F
don't al-ways say what she real - ly means.
hard lov - in' wom - an, got me feel - in' mean.
Some - times I
Some - times I

A
B♭
D
E♭
think it's a shame _ when I get feel - in' bet - ter when I'm
think it's a shame _ when I get feel - in' bet - ter when I'm
E5
F
feel - in' no pain. _
feel - in' no pain. _
Some - times I think it's a shame _ when I
Sun - down, you bet - ter take care _ if I
get feel - in' bet - ter when I'm
find you bin creep - in' round
To Coda
feel - in' no pain. _
D. S. al Coda
I can

Coda
E5
F
A
B♭
my back stairs._
Sun - down, you bet-ter take care_ if I
D
E♭
E5
F
find you bin creep-in' round_ my back stairs._
Some-times I
A
B♭
D
E♭
E5
F
think it's a sin_ when I feel like I'm win-nin' when I'm los-in' a - gain._
A
B♭
D
E♭
E5
F

SPACE ODDITY

Words and Music by
DAVID BOWIE

Moderately slow ♩ = 72
Fmaj7
Em
p
mp
Verse:
C
Ground con - trol to Ma - jor Tom.

C
Em
Ground con - trol to Ma - jor Tom.
Am
Am/G
D/F♯
Take your pro - tein pills and put your hel - met on.
C
Em
Ground con - trol to Ma - jor Tom.
C
Em
Am
Am/G
Com-menc - ing count-down, en - gines on.
Check ig - ni-tion and may

D/F♯
C9(♯11)
God's love be with you.
cresc.
Chorus:
C
E7
This is ground con - trol to Ma - jor Tom. You've real - ly made the grade.
mf
F
Fm
C/E
And the pa - pers want to know whose shirts you wear.
F
Fm
C
Now it's time to leave the cap - sule if you dare.

F
C
This is Ma - jor Tom to ground con - trol.
E7
F
I'm step-ping through the door,
and I'm
Fm
C/E
F
float - ing in a most pe - cu - liar way,
and the stars
Fm
C/E
F
look ver - y dif - fer - ent to - day.
For

Bridge:

Fmaj7 Em7

here am I sit - ting in a tin can,
Here am I float - ing 'round my tin can,

Fmaj7 Em7

far a - bove the world.
far a - bove the moon.

B♭maj7 Am G F

Plan - et Earth is blue and there's noth - ing I can do.

C F G A C F G A

Fmaj7
Em7
A
(Inst. solo ad lib.…
C
To Coda
D/E
E
Chorus:
C
E7
Though I'm past one hun - dred thou - sand miles,
I'm feel - ing ver - y still,
F
Fm
C
3
and I think my space - ship knows which way to go.

F
Fm
C/E
F
Tell my wife I love her ver - y much. She knows.
G
E7
Am
Am/G
Ground con - trol to Ma - jor Tom. Your cir - cuit's dead. There's some - thing wrong. Can you
D/F♯
C
hear me, Ma - jor Tom? Can you hear me, Ma - jor Tom? Can you
D.S. 𝄋 al Coda
𝄌 Coda
G
hear me, Ma - jor Tom? Can you…
D/E
E

UNCLE JOHN'S BAND

Words by
ROBERT HUNTER

Music by
JERRY GARCIA

Moderately
G
D
C
D
G
D
mp
C
D
G
Well, the first days — are — the hard-est days; — don't you
buck danc - er's — choice — my friend; — bet - ter
C
G
wor - ry an - y-more. 'Cause — when life — looks like Eas - y Street, there is
take — my — ad-vice. You know — all the rules by now — and the

Uncle John's Band - 7 - 1

C
G
Am
Em
dan - ger at your door.
fire from the ice.
Think this through with me;
Will you come with me?
D
Let me know your mind.
Won't you come with me?
Wo, oh, what I want to know
Wo, oh, what I want to know:
is, are you kind?
will you come with me?
1.
It's a
2.
God damn, well I de - clare,
have you seen the like?

D
C
Their walls are built of can - non - balls; their
G
D
C
D
G
C
mot-to is: "Don't tread on me."
Come hear Un - cle John's Band
mp
Am
G
D
C
play - ing to the tide.
Come with me or go a - lone, he's
G
D
C
D
G
D
C
D
come to take his chil - dren home.
It's

G
C
G
— the same sto - ry the crow told me, — it's the on - ly one — he knows.
I live in a sil - ver mine — and I call it Beg - gar's Tomb.
Like the morn - ing — sun you come — and —
I got — me a vi - o - lin — and I
C
G
Am
like the wind — you go. Ain't no time — to hate, —
beg you call — the tune. An - y - bod - y's choice, —
Em
C
D
— bare - ly time — to wait. —
— I can hear — your voice. —

C D G Am G D
Wo, oh, what I want to know: where does the
Wo, oh, what I want to know: how does the
G G C
time go? Come hear Un - cle John's Band
song go? Come hear Un - cle John's Band
mp-mf
Am G D C
by the riv - er-side. Got some things to talk a - bout-
play - ing to the tide. Come on a - long or go a - lone, he's
1. 2.
G D C D C D
here be - side the ris - ing tide. dren home.
come to take his chil -

Dm7
C
Dsus2
C(add D)
Wo, oh, what I want to know: how does the
G
Tacet
song go? Come hear Un - cle John's Band
Drums
by the riv - er - side. Got some things to talk a - bout

G
here be-side the ris - ing tide.
Come hear Un-
C
Am
D
cle John's Band playing to the tide.
Come on a-long or go
a-lone, he's come to take his chil-dren home.
Dm7
Da da da da da da,
da da da da da da.
Dsus2

TAKE IT EASY

Words and Music by
JACKSON BROWNE and GLENN FREY

Moderate Country feeling
G
C/G
Am7/G
mf
G
G
Well, I'm a - run - nin' down the road try'n' to
D
C
loos - en my load, I've got sev - en wom - en on my mind, four
G
D
C
that wan - na own me, two that wan - na stone me, one says she's a friend of mine.

G
Em
C
Take it eas - y, take it eas -
G
Am
C
Em
y, don't let the sound of your own wheels drive you cra - zy.
C
G
C
Light-en up while you still can, don't e-ven try to un-der-stand,
G
Am
C
G
just find a place to make your stand and take it eas -

G
D
C
Em
y.
Well, I'm a - stand-in' on a cor-ner in Wins-
low, Ar - i - zo - na and such a fine sight to see,
it's a girl,
my Lord, in a flat bed Ford slow-in' down to take a look at me.
Come on, ba - by,
don't say may - be,

G
Am
C
Em
I got-ta know if your sweet love is gon-na save me.
C
G
C
We may lose and we may win, though we will nev-er be here a-gain,
G
Am
C
G
so o-pen up, I'm climb-in' in, so take it eas -
G
y. Well, I'm a - run-nin' down the road try'n' to loos-en my load, got a world

D
Am7
G
of trou-ble on my mind,
look - in' for a lov-er who won't
D
C
G
Em
blow my cov-er, she's so hard to find.
Take it eas -
C
G
Am
y, take it eas - y,
don't let the sound of your own
C
Em
C
wheels make you cra - zy.
Come on, ba - by,

G
C
G
Am
don't_ say_ may - be, I got-ta know if your_ sweet_love_
C
G
Tacet
C
G
is gon-na save me._
C
G
G9
C
Oh,_we got it eas - y,
G
G9
C
Em
we ought-a take it eas - y.
R. H.

TAKE ME HOME, COUNTRY ROADS

Words and Music by
JOHN DENVER, BILL DANOFF
and TAFFY NIVERT

Moderate country two-beat 𝅗𝅥 = 82
A
mf
Verse:
F♯m
1. Al-most Heav - en, West Vir - gin - ia,
2. All my mem - 'ries gath - er 'round her,
E
D
A
Blue Ridge Moun - tains, Shen - an - do - ah Riv - er.
min - er's la - dy, strang - er to blue wa - ter.
F♯m
Life is old there, old - er than the
Dark and dust - y, paint - ed on the

E
D
trees, youn - ger than the moun - tains, grow - in' like a breeze.
sky, mist - y taste of moon - shine, tear - drop in my eye.
Chorus:
A
A
E
Coun - try roads, take me home
F#m
D
to the place I be - long.
A
E
West Vir - gin - ia, moun - tain ma - ma,

D
A
To Coda
take me home,
coun - try roads.
1.
2.
Bridge:
F♯m
E
I hear her voice in the morn-
A
D
A
in' hour; she calls me. The ra - di - o re - minds me of my
E
F♯m
G
home far a - way. And driv - in' down the road, I get a

D
A
E
feel - in' that I should have been home yes - ter - day,
E7
D.S. 𝄋 al Coda
yes - ter - day.
Coun - try roads,
Coda
E
A
Take me home,
coun - try roads.
E
A
D/E
A
Take me home,
coun - try roads.

THUNDER ROAD

Words and Music by
BRUCE SPRINGSTEEN

Freely
F
Am
Dm
F
B♭
mp legato
(with pedal)
Moderately fast ♩ = 138
F
Am
B♭
Csus
C
1.The
Verse 1:
F
C
F
B♭
C
B♭
F
C7
F
C7
screen door slams,_ Mar - y's_ dress_ waves;_ like a
F
C
F
C
B♭
vi-sion she danc - es a - cross the porch_ as the ra-di-o plays._ Roy

C Bb C Bb C F C F Bb
Or-bi-son's sing - in' for the lone - ly. Hey, that's me, and I want_ you on - ly. Don't turn me
F C7 F C Dm C Bb/C C7
home_ a - gain._ I just___ can't face__ my - self___ a - lone___ a-gain. Don't
F C7 F Bb C Bb F C7 F C7
run back in - side,_ dar-ling, you know just what I'm here___ for._ So you're scared_
mf
F C7 F C Bb
___ and you're think-ing that may-be we ain't_ that young_ an - y - more._ Show a lit-tle

C7
B♭
C7
B♭
C7
F
C7
F
B♭
F
faith, there's mag - ic in the night.
You ain't a beau-ty, but hey, you're al - right.
B♭
F/B♭
C7
F
C7
F
C7
Oh, and that's al - right with me.
2. You can hide
Verse 2:
F
Dm
F
B♭
'neath your cov-ers and stud-y your pain, make cross-es from your lov-ers, throw ros-es in the rain,
F
Am
B♭
B♭/C
C7
waste your sum-mer pray-ing in vain for a sav - ior to rise from these streets.
Well now, I'm

F
Dm
F
B♭
C
no he-ro, that's un-der-stood. All the re-demp-tion I can of-fer, girl, is be-neath this dirt-y hood,
F
Am
B♭
B♭/C
C
with a chance to make it good some-how. Hey, what else can we do now, ex-cept roll
Pre-chorus 1:
F
B♭
F
down the win-dow and let the wind blow back your hair. Well, the
Am
B♭
night's bust-ing o-pen, these two lanes will take us an-y-where. We got

C
B♭/D
C/E
F
Gm
F/A
B♭
C
one last chance_ to make it real,_ to trade_ in these wings_ on some_ wheels.
B♭
F/A
Gm
F
C/E
Dm
C
B♭
Dm
C
Dm
B♭/D
C7
Climb in_ back, heav - en's_ wait-ing down on_ the tracks._
Chorus:
F
Dm
F
B♭
Oh, oh,_ come take_ my hand,_ rid-ing out to-night to_ case the prom-ised land.
F
Am
B♭
C
Oh,_ oh,_ Thun-der Road, oh,_ Thun-der Road, oh,_ Thun-der Road.

F Dm F B♭

Ly-ing out there like a kill-er in the sun. Hey, I know it's late, we can ___ make it if we run.

F Am B♭ C

Oh, ___ Thun-der Road, sit tight, _ take hold, ___ Thun-der

F F/A B♭ *Bridge:* C6 C9

Road. ___ Well, I got ___ this gui-tar and I learned how to make it talk. _

mf

F Dm

___ And my car's out back if you're read-y to take _ that

B♭maj7
C
B♭
C
long walk from your front porch to my front seat. The door's
Am
Dm
B♭
Dm
Gm
B♭/F
o-pen, but the ride ain't free, and I know you're lone-ly for words that I ain't spo-ken, but to-
Pre-chorus 2:
Csus
F
B♭
night we'll be free. All the prom - is-es-'ll be bro-ken. There were ghosts in the eyes of all the boys you
F
Am
sent a-way. They haunt this dust - y beach road in the skel-e-ton frames of burned

B♭ C

out Chev - ro - lets. They scream your name at night in the street, your grad - u - a - tion

F B♭ Am

gown lies in rags at their feet. And in the lone - ly cool be - fore dawn, you hear their

B♭ Gm F C/E Dm C B♭ Am

en - gines roar - ing on. But when you get to the porch, they're gone on the

B♭ Gm

wind. So, Mar - y, climb in. It's a town

B♭
C
F
N.C.
full of los - ers. I'm pull-ing out of here to win.
8va
cresc.
ff
Instrumental:
F
C
F
B♭
Tenor Sax.:
3
f
F
C
B♭
C
F
C
F

B♭ F C

B♭ F/A Gm F C B♭ Am Gm C7

F C F B♭

F C B♭ C

Repeat ad lib. and fade

THE WEIGHT

Words and Music by
ROBBIE ROBERTSON

Moderately slow 𝅗𝅥 = 72 (♩♪ = ♩𝅘𝅥𝅮 triplet)

N.C.

mf

A

Verse:

A C♯m

1. I pulled in - to Naz - a-reth, was
2.–5. *See additional lyrics*

D A C♯m

feel - in' 'bout half past dead. I just need some-place__ where

D A C♯m

I__ can lay__ my head.____ "Hey, mis-ter, can you tell me where a

A C#m

man_ might find a bed?"__ He just grinned and shook my hand._

D A *Chorus:* E D

"No,"_ was all__ he said. Take a load off, Fan - ny.

straight eighths *sim.*

A E D A E D

Take a load for free.________ Take a load off, Fan - ny.

And, and__________ you put the load right on

And__________ you put the load right on me.

A
E
F♯m
E
1.2.3.
D
me.
4.
D
A
E
F♯m
E
D
5.
D
A
E
F♯m
E
D

Verse 2:
I picked up my bag, I went lookin' for a place to hide,
When I saw Carmen and the devil walkin' side by side.
I said, "Hey, Carmen, come on, let's go downtown."
He said, "I gotta go, but my friend can stick around."
(To Chorus:)

Verse 3:
Go down, Miss Moses, there's nothing that you can say.
It's just old Luke and Luke's waitin' on the Judgment Day.
I said, "Luke, my friend, what about young Anna Lee?"
He said, "Do me a favor, son, won't you stay and keep Anna Lee company."
(To Chorus:)

Verse 4:
Crazy Chester followed me and he caught me in the fog.
He said, "I'll fix your rack if you'll take Jack, my dog."
I said, "Wait a minute, Chester, you know I'm a peaceful man."
He said, "That's okay, boy, won't you feed him when you can."
(To Chorus:)

Verse 5:
Catch a cannonball, now, take me down the line.
My bag is sinkin' low and I do believe it's time
To get back to Miss Fanny, you know she's the only one
Who sent me here with her regards for everyone.
(To Chorus:)

WEREWOLVES OF LONDON

Words and Music by
WARREN ZEVON, WADDY WACHTEL
and LEROY MARINELL

Moderately ♩ = 108
D
C
G
mf
Verse 1 (sing 1st time only):
1. I saw a were - wolf with a Chi - nese men - u in his hand
Verse 2 (sing 2nd time only):
2. If you hear him howl - ing a-round your kitch-en door,
sim.
walk - ing through the streets of So - ho in the rain.
you bet - ter not let him in.

D
C
G
He was look-ing for a place called Lee Ho Fook's,
Lit-tle old la-dy got mu-ti-lat-ed late last night,
D
C
G
gon-na get a big dish of beef chow mein.
were - wolves of Lon - don a - gain.
Chorus:
D
C
G
D
C
A - woo, were - wolves of Lon - don, a - woo!

G
D
C
G
A - woo, were - wolves of Lon - don,
To Coda
1.
2.
D
C
G
G
a - woo!
Huh!
Guitar solo ad lib.:
D
C
G
D
C
1.
G
2.
G
3. He's the
…end solo)

Verse 3:
D
C
G
hair - y - head - ed gent who ran a - muck in Kent.
mf
Late - ly he's been o - ver - heard in May - fair.
You bet - ter stay a - way from him.
He'll rip your lungs out, Jim.
D.S. 𝄋 al Coda
Huh! I'd like to meet his tai - lor.

Coda

G

Verse 4:

D C

4. Well, I saw Lon Cha - ney walk -

G D C

ing with the Queen, do - ing the were - wolves of Lon - don.

G D C

I saw Lon Cha - ney, Ju - nior

G D C

walk - ing with the Queen, *uh!* do - ing the were - wolves of Lon - don.

G
D
C
I saw a were - wolf drink-ing a pi -
G
D
C
ña co - la - da at Trad - er Vics
and his hair was per - fect.
Chorus:
G
D
C
G
A - woo,
D
C
G
were - wolves of Lon-don.
Huh, draw blood.

D
C
G
A - woo,
were - wolves of Lon-don.
Repeat and fade

WILD HORSES

Words and Music by
MICK JAGGER and KEITH RICHARDS

Moderately slow ♩ = 88
G
Am7
(Lead Gtr.)
mf
G
Gsus
G
Am7
G
Gsus
G
(end Gtr.)
Verse:
Bm
G
Gsus
G
1. Child - hood liv - ing
2. I watched you suf - fer
3. I know I've dreamed you

Bm
G
Gsus
G
is eas - y to do.
a dull ach - ing pain.
a sin and a lie.
Am
G
C
D
The things you want - ed,
Now you de - cid - ed
I have my free - dom,
G
Gsus
G
D
C
I bought them for you.
to show me the same.
but I don't have much time.
Bm
G
Gsus
G
Grace - less la - dy,
No sweep-ing ex - its
Faith has been bro - ken,

Bm G Gsus G
you know who I am.
or off - stage lines
tears must be cried.
Am G C D
You know I can't let you
could make me feel bit - ter
Let's do some liv - ing
G Gsus G D
slide through my hands.
or treat you un - kind.
af - ter we die.
Chorus:
Am C D D7 G F
Wild hors - es could - n't drag me a -

To Coda
C
Bm
Am
C
D
D7
way.
Wild,
wild
hors - es
1.
G
F
C
2.
G
F
could - n't drag
me
a - way.
could - n't drag
me
a -
C
F(9)
C
way.
(Gtr. solo…
F(9)
C
D
G
Gsus
G
…end solo)

3.
G
F
C
we'll ride them some - day.
Solo:
Bm
G
Gsus
G
Bm
G
Gsus
G
(Lead Gtr.)
p
Am
G
C
D
G
Gsus
G
D
D.S. % al Coda
G/D
(end Gtr.)
mf
Coda
G
F
C
G
we'll ride them some - day.

WISH YOU WERE HERE

Words and Music by
ROGER WATERS and DAVID GILMOUR

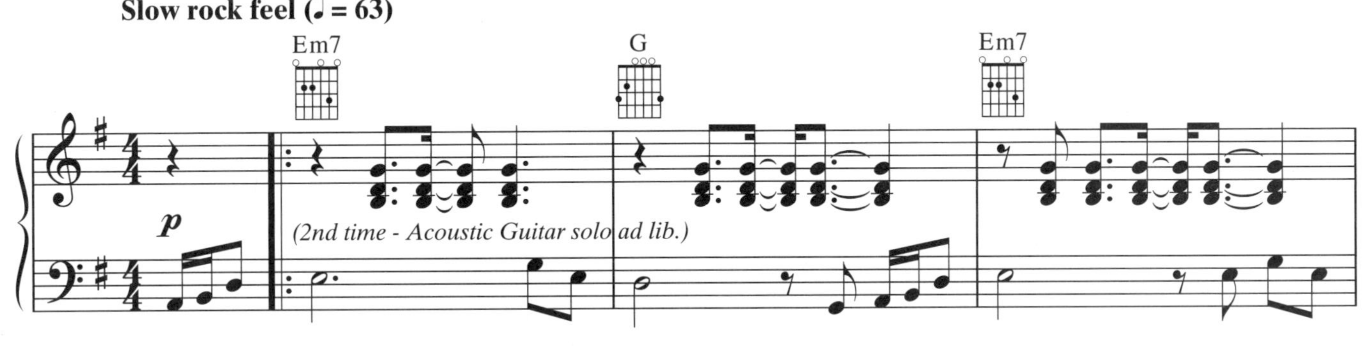
Slow rock feel (♩ = 63)
Em7
G
Em7
p
(2nd time - Acoustic Guitar solo ad lib.)

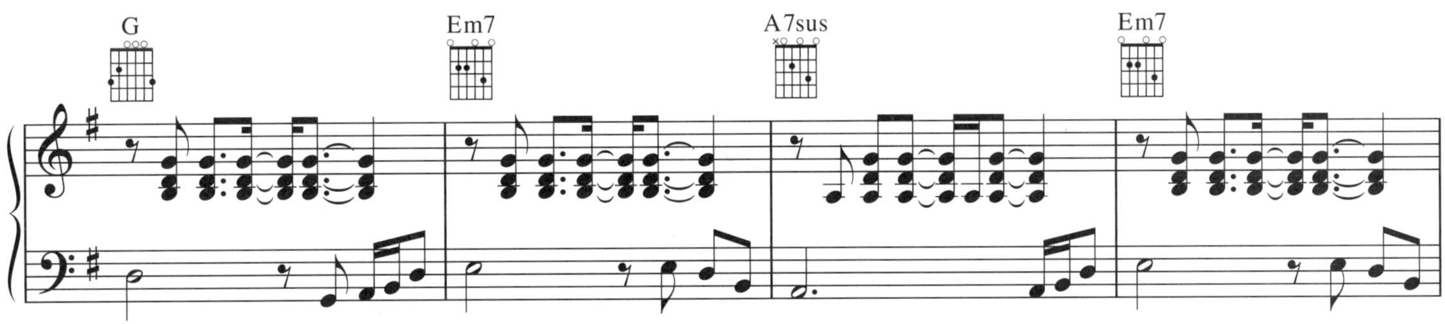
G
Em7
A7sus
Em7

A7sus
1.
G
2.
G
(end solo)

Verse 1:
C
D
So, so you think you can tell heav - en from hell,
mp

Am
G
blue skys__ from pain.___
Can you tell a green field_
D/F♯
C
from a cold_ steel rail?___
A smile_ from a veil?_
Am
G
Do you think you can tell?___
Did they get you to trade_
mf
Verse 2:
C
D
your he - roes for ghosts?___
Hot ash - es for trees?_

Am
G
Hot air for a cool breeze?
Cold com-fort for change?
D/F♯
C
And did you ex-change a walk-on part in the war
Am
G
Em7
for a lead role in a cage?
Dobro solo ad lib.
dim.
mp
G
Em7
G
Em7

A7sus
Em7
A7sus
G
cresc.
Chorus:
C
D
How I wish, how I wish you were here. We're just
mf
Am
G
two lost souls swim-ming in a fish bowl, year af - ter year,
D
C
run-ning o - ver the same old ground. What have we found? The same old

Am G

fears. Wish you were here.

Ending:

Em G Em

(2nd time - Dobro doubled by scat vocal cont.)

mp

G Em A

Em A G

Repeat and fade

(1st time - Dobro doubled by scat vocal)

YOU CAN'T ALWAYS GET WHAT YOU WANT

Guitar in Open E tuning *(optional w/ Capo at 8th fret)*:
⑥ = E ③ = G♯
⑤ = B ② = B
④ = E ① = E

Words and Music by
MICK JAGGER and KEITH RICHARDS

Moderately ♩ = 104
N.C.
(Boys Choir) mp
I saw her to-day at the re - cep - tion, a glass of wine in her
(Choir) Aah, aah, aah,

hand. I know she would meet her con - nec - tion, at her feet was a foot-loose
aah. Aah, aah, aah,

man. No, you can't al - ways get what you want. You can't al - ways get what you
aah. Aah, aah, aah,

want.__ You can't al - ways get what you want.__ And if you
aah. Aah, aah,
F C
try some time___ you'll find___ you get what you need.
(Guitar)
aah, aah, aah.
mp
C2 C C2 C C2 C C2 C F
(French Horn)
C2 * (Cont. chord pattern throughout) F C2

F
C2
F
(Lead Vocal) 1. I
Verses 1 & 5:
C2
F
saw her to - day at the re - cep - tion,
5. See additional lyrics
C2
F
a glass of wine in her hand. I knew
C2
F
she was gon - na meet her con - nec - tion. At her

C2
F
feet was a foot - loose man.
You
Chorus:
C2
F
can't al - ways get what you want.
You
C2
F
can't al - ways get what you want.
You
C2
F
To Coda
can't al - ways get what you want.
But if you

D
F
C7
try some - times,
well, you might
find
you get what you
need.
Oh,
F
C7
F
yeah.
2. And I went
Verses 2, 3, & 4:
C2
F
down
to the
dem - on
-
stra
-
tion
to
get
3. 4. See additional lyrics
C2
F
my
fair
share
of
a
-
buse.
Sing - in', "We're

C2 F

___ gon - na vent___ our frus - tra - tion.______ If we don't,_

C2 F

1. 3. *To Next Strain*

___ we're gon - na blow a fif - ty - amp fuse."________ *Sing it to me, now.* You

2. F

Chorus:

C7

________ 4. We de - cid - can't al - ways get what you want._

F7 C7

__________ You can't al - ways get what you want._

F7
C7
F7
You can't al - ways get what you want.
But if you
D
F
try some - times,
well, you just might find,
you get what you
1.
C7
F7
C7
need.
Oh
ba - by,
yeah.
F7
2.
C7
F7
3. I
need.
Oh,
yeah.
Whoo!

D7sus/A
D7sus/B
D7sus/C
(Choir) Aah,
aah,
D7sus
D7sus/G
aah,
aah.
Chorus:
C7
F7
C7
Aah,
aah,
aah,
F7
C7
F7
aah,
aah,
aah.

D
10
F
8
C7
8
You get what you need.
F7
8
C7
8
F7
8
D.S. al Coda
5. I
Coda
D
10
F
8
try some-time, you just might find, you just might find you get what you
C7
8
F7
8
need.
(Choir) Aah,
aah,

C7 F7

aah, aah.

C7 F7

Aah, aah,

C7 F7

Repeat ad lib. and fade

aah.

Verse 3:
I went down to the Chelsea drugstore
To get your prescription filled.
I was standin' in line with Mr. Jimmy.
A-man, did he look pretty ill.

Verse 4:
We decided that we would have a soda;
My favorite flavor, cherry red,
I sung my song to Mr. Jimmy.
Yeah, and he said one word to me, and that was "dead."
I said to him…
(To Chorus:)

Verse 5:
I saw her today at the reception.
In her glass was a bleeding man.
She was practiced at the art of deception.
Well, I could tell by her blood-stained hands.
Say it!
(To Chorus:)

YOU AND ME

Words and Music by
JASON WADE and JUDE COLE

Moderately slow ♩. = 52
G5
C2
D(4)/F♯
G/B
Em7
Dsus
mf
Verse:
C(9)
C2
G5
C2
D(4)/F♯
1. What day is it, and in what
2. All of the things that I want to
G/B
Em7
Dsus
C(9)
C2
month? This clock nev - er seemed so a - live.
say just are - n't com - ing out right. I'm
G5
C2
D(4)/F♯
G/B
Em7
I can't keep up, and I can't back down. I've been los - ing
trip - ping on words. You got my head spin - ning. I don't know where to

Dsus C(9) C2

so much time. / go from here. 'Cause it's

Chorus:

G Am7 C(9) Em7

you and me and all of the peo - ple with noth - ing to do,

G Em7 D G Am7

noth - ing to { lose. / prove. } And it's you and me and

C(9) Em7 G Em7

all of the peo - ple, and I don't know why I can't keep my

1.
D
C(9)
eyes off of you.
2.
D
G
Bridge:
Bm
eyes off of you.
Some - thing a - bout
C
G
D
Em7
you now,
I can't quite fig - ure out.
Am7
D
Ev - 'ry - thing she does is beau - ti - ful.

Bm
Cm
Ev - 'ry - thing she does is right.
'Cause it's
Chorus:
G
Am7
C(9)
Em7
G
you and me and all of the peo - ple with noth - ing to do,
Em7
D
G
Am7
C(9)
noth - ing to { lose. prove. } And it's you and me and all of the peo -
Em7
G
Em7
1.
D
ple, and I don't know why I can't keep my eyes off of

2.
D
G5
C2
D(4)/F♯
eyes off of you.
G/B
Em7
Dsus
C(9)
G5
C2
D(4)/F♯
What day is it, and in what
G/B
Em7
Dsus
C(9)
month? This clock nev - er seemed so a - live.